How Elite Advisors GROW!

PROVEN, TRUST-BASED, MARKETING
for FINANCIAL ADVISORS
Be Better, Do Better
& Get More Clients

By Two Time National Best Selling Author
Mitchell Levin, MD, CWPP, CAPP
The Financial Physician™

With **Kyle A. Levin, JD**

Other books by Dr. Mitchell Levin

Power Principles for Success

Goal! The Financial Physician's Ultimate Survival Guide for the Professional Athlete

Shift Happens

Smart Choices for Serious Money

Cover Your Assets: How to Build, Protect and Maintain Your Own Financial Fortress

Table of Contents

FORWARD

Dear Reader,

Thank you for taking the time to read this book. Since you are reading this, you seek to improve. You must be good for your clients, then. I encourage any financial advisor who desires more clients, and more fun, to read this book.

You, of course, are a busy professional, and finding spare time to do anything can be difficult. That being said, I believe that the ideas contained in this book will help you run a more efficient practice, and will help you become a more dominant financial marketing success story.

We are bombarded with advice every day, some of it good, and some of it bad. Sometimes it can be hard to decide whom to listen to. I am sure that you are asking yourself, what makes this book so special? The methods contained in this book are proven. I have read numerous books on the subject of marketing, and while some are better than others, this book differentiates itself from all the other books out there because of its use of *trust-based marketing*.

A lot of books give advice on how to market your financial advisor business utilizing radio or television. While I believe that this book will offer you excellent guidance on these topics, the real value of this book is that it will help you become a better financial advisor by using the *language of trust.* Trust is essential in any partnership, and if you utilize the tips given in this book, you will be on your way to building a stronger relationship with your existing clients and becoming more effective in converting prospective clients into actual clients.

You will also gain practical knowledge in such varied topics as Internet marketing, newsletters, public relations, television advertisements, and a whole host of other topics, tools and tactics. Today's marketplace is tough. There are hundreds of thousands of financial advisors throughout this country, each one competing against the others to sign up prospective clients. It is not enough to rely solely on one form of marketing any more. In order to be competitive, you need to be a master, or at least highly competent in all of the disciplines. This book serves as a *practical guide* to achieving just that.

This book will also offer you guidance on how you can differentiate yourself from your competition. Have you ever noticed that most financial advisors' marketing material looks the same? If all financial advisors look the same to a prospective client, than there is no real reason why a prospective client should choose one advisor over any other. This book will give you the blueprint to help you identify the clients that you want, and position yourself differently from the rest of the financial advisors out there so that you become the go-to financial advisor in your area.

Some of the ideas contained in this book may seem foreign, or even counter intuitive to you. You think to yourself, "I've been doing all right up to this point, why should I change." Do not be afraid of trying something different. It's a new world out there, technologically speaking, and innovations are happening every day. If you do not continue to update your skill set, and strive to improve your marketing techniques, it will not be long until you find yourself outdated and outgunned by financial advisors who are constantly innovating. So, take a chance. Nothing says that you need to implement every idea in this book right away. You can start with one tweak to your marketing program and build on that foundation.

I hope that you are able to take the advice written in this book and use it to remake your practice into the best it can be. Keep in mind as you are reading this book that Summit Wealth Partners, Inc. are experts in marketing and are there to help with strategic advice and planning on a whole host of issues. Feel free to call them if you have any questions.

In closing, strive to be an innovator. Take the steps that others are not. Constantly be looking for the next great marketing technique and work on improving the skills that you have accumulated already. Follow the techniques that you learn in this book and you will see results. And enjoy your newly-found success.

To your clients, and to your success,

Kyle A. Levin, JD

Introduction
Do You Have ACE?

How many of you believe that Suze Orman is the best financial advisor in the country? You may be snickering. We all believe that we are far better financial planners than her, but I want you to think about this. If she were to come into your town today, and take out a full page ad that says, "Saturday morning I'm going to be hosting an event at the arena," do you really believe that she would not be able to fill that arena with 20,000 people, and that she would not have a line around the block with people waiting to get in?

Even if she chose to charge $15,000 for financial planning, would she still not have a long line of people willing to pay her price? If she also said that she had an investment management platform, I am willing to bet that she would be able to collect $1 billion in one day in your town. Many of us believe that this would happen.

So how did Suze Orman get to where she is?

It's what I call ACE.

The A stands for Authority, the C stands for Celebrity and the E stands for Exclusivity. Let's examine this in more detail. Authority – the root word of authority is the word author. If you become an author, you're automatically an authority. Celebrity – how do you become a celebrity?

Well, it begins with first writing a book and we can show you how to write a book. In fact, you can all write a book and you all should write a book. It doesn't take that long. It does take a lot of work. It's very simple, but simple isn't easy. This book will help you get started and finish strong.

So you establish your authority by publishing a book, and then what do you do? Well, you don't just let it sit there. A book is one of the best business cards you could ever have, and there are multiple ways for you to repurpose your book through webinars, white papers, articles and other avenues. Create podcasts and webinars from you book. Make a YouTube video that features your book. This will put you on the path to becoming a local celebrity. Submit what you produce to your local press. They are always on the lookout for interesting content. You will also want to submit your material to local television stations, radio shows, and be sure to promote your book through advertisements.

Once you have become an authority by publishing your book, how do you become a celebrity, and why should you strive to become a celebrity? When you promote your book, you will be using an advertisement of some sort, whether it's through direct mail or newspaper or radio. What you are trying to do is breakdown threshold resistance.

Threshold Resistance is a concept popularized by Alfred Taubman. You may remember his name. He's probably most well known for developing the modern American shopping mall. In the old days, a storefront would have a sidewalk and then there would be this little kiosk in the middle of the sidewalk, and you would have to walk around this kiosk to get to the door to get inside the store

What Alfred Taubman discovered was that if you get rid of that kiosk and move the front door right up to the sidewalk, more people would enter the store. Every single store in every single mall now uses this concept. That is threshold resistance.

As financial advisors, what do we try to do? Usually we say, "Hey, come on in and become a client," or maybe it's one step less, "Come on in for a free consultation." This is way too much work and way too much risk for most prospective clients. In fact, why do you think we like to shop online? We don't want the human interaction because we're afraid we're going to get sold. We all want to buy, but nobody wants to get sold.

We are in an understandably untrusting time. By publishing your book, and making yourself a celebrity, you will help people know you better, and help breakdown threshold resistance.

How do you create *exclusivity*, the E in ACE? I have friends who only work with retirees from AT&T and they've been able to generate an enormous amount of business. I have friends who only work with physicians. Somebody I know only works with small business owners. In fact, I've got a friend who brings in over $90 million a year by himself with a couple of sub-producers by only working with retirees. It can be done. That is exclusive.

Let's talk about ACE and your positioning. Now you may be wondering why I have an MD after my name. It does not stand for Managing Director. What it does stand for is Medical Doctor. I was an eye surgeon, which was a great profession. Society held me in very high regard. In terms of regard, just below doctors are attorneys and accountants and just below them are used car salesmen and just below used car salesmen are those of us in the financial industry. It hurts, I know, and why is that? It could be because too many of us do not put our clients' interests ahead of our own. It could be that we do not use the language of trust, which I will cover shortly.

Of course, you *really want to grow* your practice. I presume that is the real reason you are reading this book. How many of you know an advisor whose practice has basically hit a ceiling? Their growth has diminished. Could it be that doing it yourself, especially portfolio management (and the dreadful "back office" headache) is one big reason you have not grown?

Ask yourself this question, "Why should a potential client work with you as opposed to any other financial advisor out there?" This is an extremely difficult question to answer. Here are the three answers you may not use. You may not say "quality", you may not say "service", and you may not say the level of "care" that you provide, because everyone seems to *say* these. Answering this question is not easy, is it? This book can help you with this answer, to differentiate yourself. So you can...

Be better. Do better. And get more clients.

PART I:
MOVING YOUR MINDSET TO THE LANGUAGE OF TRUST

"Seek First to Understand, then to be understood"

or "Where is the Beef?"

Chapter 1
The Language of Trust

The language of trust is expressed in your actions. The language of trust includes punctuality. So when you say you will deliver something, why not deliver by overnight courier? And it includes something called authenticity. Make sure your primary purpose is to help others first. That will get you what you want. People have a strong sense of when you care about yourself first. It also includes your means and content of your communications.

If it is true that we are living in untrusting times, how do we get people to trust us and establish that trust quickly? You have to have integrity. You have to be able to communicate your integrity to potential clients. You have to be able to do it without putting competitors down, or disparaging things that you may disagree with. Does it make a client feel good to learn that a fee only advisor thinks that commission only advisors are no good?

What clients are *not* buying is… your product. They are buying *you*. The language of trust begins with integrity. I define integrity as doing what you say when you say it. The best way to show integrity is to be on time. The second best way to show integrity is to deliver more than what you promised. When I come out of a meeting, the first thing I do is I write a handwritten note thanking that person for the meeting. I then send an email *immediately* after the client or the referring center of influence has left the office.

Newsletter?

Why is the language of trust so important, and how can you maintain it? Let me ask you this question; how many of you deliver a newsletter to your clients, your prospective clients and your referring centers of influence? How many of you deliver your newsletters by hard mail? How many of you send them electronically? How many of you think that your newsletters are being read? How many of you are developing referrals and retention and reward and recognition through your newsletters? Remember these four R's; referrals, recognition, reward and retention. Have you quantified these numbers?

Now you may have heard "that half of all marketing is wasted, you just don't know which half". This approach may be fine when you are brand building, but it is not so great when you are a small or even midsize financial advisor. A large corporation like Pepsi can afford to brand build. If you are Merrill Lynch you can afford to brand build. As a smaller player, we've got to have direct response marketing. We need to know that if we are spending $6,000 on a marketing campaign, we are able to generate a return of at least $18,000. Why? Because when we spend scarce resources on marketing, it has to return value. You need to know this. You need to quantify this. How can you do that?

You can start to do this with a newsletter. In fact, if there is only one thing you do, send out a customized, hard-copy, mailed newsletter.

SUMMIT WEALTH
— PARTNERS —

Volume 5, Issue 8, September 2014

The Rational  Optimist™

That's It; It's Over

by Mitch Levin, MD CWPP, CAPP

I just couldn't believe it. No matter how prepared you think you are, you are never fully prepared. Mom passed away during the early morning hours of June 20, 2014. My wife Swantje reminded me that she had only lived five days longer than her mother. Of course, Dad was all broken up. And you can imagine all the emotions and heartache that surrounded me and my family.

Mom was a very passionate and emotional lady. And I understand, for those of you that know me, it may be hard to believe, because I am so logical. She was a delightful, fun, intelligent, warm, loving, giving person. Family was most important to her and she was a good mother, a terrific mother-in-law to my wife, and a fantastic and involved grandmother, as well as, an exceedingly appreciative wife to my dad

Mom and I didn't always see eye to eye, but I am very thankful that for the last 30 years we had a very good relationship. In fact, I'm really grateful that I had driv-

Barbara (1951-2014) and Jess Levin

en to Deerfield to have dinner with Mom just a couple of days before she passed away. The circumstances were a little unusual. Ever since I can remember, Mom had suffered from one illness or another, and yet simultaneously, she was as healthy as a horse. Almost always happy, upbeat, and positive, Mom tried to see the good in others. During the last four or five years, Mom became depressed; perhaps it was partly due to her serious health issues that had disabled her to the point of living as a shut-in. And Dad, although healthy and fit at age 86, mostly lived as a shut-in with her.

So when a cardiologist from the University of Miami suggested a procedure that could help her heart and possibly improve her quality of life, she considered it. After years of deliberation, she finally decided that it was time for her to make the effort to undergo the procedure. I'm not sure if I would have encouraged her to do that at her age of 83. Having any type of heart procedure always includes risk. Howev-

continued on Page 6

 CHAD WARRICK
$1 A Day Can-
Make Kids Rich
Page 2

 JASON PRINT
Why Florida?
Page 3

 JEFFREY
JANSON:
Summit's New
Senior Wealth
Advisor
Page 5

September 2014, The Rational Optimist. 1

A newsletter will help you **maintain the language of trust**. We send a monthly newsletter out to all of our clients, all of our prospective clients and all of our referring centers of influence. We send it hard mail. Twice a month we take some of our newsletters and convert them into an email newsletter and once a month we produce a video newsletter. We are in constant communication with our prospective clients, reinforcing the language of trust. We are also able to measure how many clients we get from the newsletter and what the cost is to us. It's expensive. It takes a lot of effort. It's hard work. But hard work pays off.

One of the worst things you can do in any kind of marketing is to be boring. That's why Jim Kramer incorporates all sorts of bells and whistles into his show. Numbers tend to bore a lot of people and excessive talk about money tends to bore a lot of people. Even clients who are serious about their money get fatigued when the only thing you talk about is money. Make sure your newsletter is interesting.

What radio station do you listen to? What radio station do you think your clients listen to? All your clients are listening to the same radio station. It's the only radio station they ever listen to. The radio station is WIIFM. That stands for **What's In It For Me.** That's it. They don't care that you want to grow your practice. They don't care that you want this to be the best year ever. They don't want to help you. They just want to know what's in it for them. If you cannot persuade them of your value proposition, if you cannot show them that working with you is worth it, they are not going to continue to work with you. Correct? This too can be done through your newsletter.

Recently we received a call from somebody we hadn't heard from in four years. This woman had gone to one of our seminars. She had primarily lived on social security, and one day she comes into the office and says, "Chad, I've got some land. As soon as I sell my land I'll have a little bit of money. I'd like to invest it with you." Who knew exactly what she had? We sent her a newsletter followed by another one and then another one. We must have sent her four years of newsletters. Recently we heard from her. "Chad, my properties are selling. It looks like I'm going to net out $30 million. I want you to handle my money." Did the newsletter cause that? No. Did the newsletter help? Yes.

I will give you another example. I get a call out of the blue from someone I met at a golf course out of state. He tells me, " Mitch, I'm selling my business. It's going to be in the tens of millions of dollars. I want to sit down and talk with you." I had not seen him in about a year and a half, but he had been receiving our newsletters all that time. These are not rare opportunities. Things like this happen over and over again. A newsletter is a crucial component of any marketing strategy.

Here is a truth about the state of the world; everybody has commoditized what everybody else has done. Do we need another money manager? Do we need another financial advisor? Do we need another bank? Another hamburger stand? We have an abundance of everything. We don't need any of it. We want it, we don't need it.

So how do you distinguish yourself as a financial advisor since we are all commoditized? Clients expect that you are going to create a pretty decent portfolio for them. They expect that their portfolio is going to be efficient. They expect that it's going to have proper performance. They also expect that you are going to deliver to them the appropriate service level. With the advent of low cost internet-based allocation firms and their increase in popularity, the landscape has become even more challenging. You really need to be able to distinguish yourself.

One of the best ways to distinguish yourself is through the hard-copy newsletter. Your competitors are not making the effort to do this.

Closing Ratio Differentiation

A truly important way to differentiate yourself is to increase your closing ratio. Imagine the old numbers game. I would see ten prospective clients, I would book three appointments, and then I would close one client. Now I really don't like the word "closing". If you've seen Glen Gary, Glen Ross, you know the motto, "always be closing". That's the "ABC's" of selling. Well, in the language of trust, I think that's a mistake.

In fact, where in the sales process do you think you lose the client? None of us have a 100% closing ratio. I know I don't. Do we lose the client in the beginning? Do we lose the client in the middle of the process? Do we lose the client at the end? Think about it. Do people really forget to close? Here's what I think. I think we lose the client at the opening. I think we should always be opening. Turn your language into, "Mr. Smith, would you be open to a conversation?" Who is not open to something? This is a much softer approach then starting with, "what do you want, what do you need?"

I have a friend Rory who is a restaurant consultant. Here is what he told me. If a server simply delivers your check, people usually give their normal tip percentage. If the server delivers the check with a piece of candy, that tip goes up by 11%. If the server then delivers that piece of candy, turns around and says, "Oh, I really like you. You're really nice people. Here's more candy." the tip goes up by 38%.

If we are able to increase our closing ratio, then we don't have to see more people. Always strive to use the language of trust. How about this for a closer? "Mr. Smith, what would you like to do next?" As opposed to, "sign here, and press hard because the home office needs a copy." Unfortunately, that is what potential clients have come to expect. They expect you to be closing. When you go to a store, it does not matter what type of store, and a salesperson comes up to you and says, "May I help you?" What do you say? "Sorry, I am just looking."

We are there to buy. We don't just go to the store because we have nothing else to do. I know that personally, I would rather be playing golf or hanging out with my wife or smoking a cigar, not just looking. We are never just looking. We are thinking about buying. So you have a potential client come to your office. They are there because they have a problem. They are only going to buy if you help them recognize that they have a problem, you help them recognize they want to solve that problem, and you help them recognize they want *you* to help them solve that problem. If you are unable to get them to recognize those three things, you will not have a new client.

So how are you going to increase that closing ratio? You're going to do it through the language of trust.

Ciao, Baby?

There is this little Italian restaurant in Longboat Key that I've been going to for the past 20 years. One day, I decided to order their dish, the *Frutti di Mare* as a takeout order. I asked the person taking my order if it was possible to have the mussels and clams taken out of their shells. The response was, "We are terribly busy, so I am not sure that we can do that."

I get to the restaurant to pick up my order, which was not ready yet, so I ask again, "Is the chef able to take the clams and mussels out of the shell for me?" The waiter said, "No, the chef can't do it."

Looking around, there were at least twenty tables, but only two of them were occupied. It was clear to me that they had the time to take the clams and mussels out of the shell if they wanted to, they just weren't willing. Is it any wonder that this restaurant was not crowded? They were not providing high levels of customer service. Were they willing to alienate a long-time, loyal, repeat customer?

What does this story have to do with us? A friend of mine, a terrific advisor to some supremely successful clients, BT, smartly said, "You've got to <u>close the back door, and keep it closed</u>."

What he means by this is that it doesn't really matter how many new clients you bring in the front door if you keep losing clients out the back. We all know that an existing client is the most likely to keep "buying" from us, and that keeping that client is most cost-effective, especially compared to the cost of acquisition of new clients through the "front door".

My colleague, and now partner, Jason Print, did a fantastic job of keeping the back door closed. He cobbled together two disparate, completely different practices and, over 10 years, did not lose one client. In fact, he was highly successful in raising their fees even though he was a new advisor to the firm. He did it through quality service and the language of trust.

Another colleague and partner, Chad Warrick, also figured out how to turn his portion of the junior advisory into becoming the lead advisor in the office. He did this by not only keeping the back door closed, keeping the clients exceedingly happy through high quality service; but also, through the language of trust, by obtaining a greater amount of the client's share of assets.

Keeping this back door closed is exceedingly important. You already know, at least intuitively, that client retention is the keystone to your success. And you may be aware that your best clients are continually being "pinged on" by your competitors. It is imperative then, that you let your clients know how much you appreciate them.

Provide your clients with the good service that they expect. Believe it or not, they always expect more than what you are giving them. Most clients are not high maintenance, but they are high demand and they expect unbelievable service. Give it to them. Give them more than they expect. Provide them with the proper service team and you will be able to keep that back door closed.

Without closing the back door, it doesn't really matter how many new clients you bring in because it costs a lot more time and money to bring in a new client than it does to retain an existing client.

I can't say it enough. Keep the back door closed. Don't ever hear the words, "*Ciao baby*".

Chapter 2
Are You Talking to Me?

Who is your ideal client? I want you to take a moment now and write down what your ideal client looks like. I have had people say that their ideal client is anybody with a checkbook. But let's be honest with ourselves. There is an ideal client type for every financial advisor.

I will tell you who my ideal client is. It's a 58-year-old business owner who has a net worth between $2 million and $20 million. They probably have half a million dollars in their 401k, a $2 Million investment account, a half a million dollar house and they are trying to figure out their $15 million dollar business.

They want to know when they can retire, and whether or not they are going to be able to maintain the lifestyle they have become accustomed to. I've got to tell you, you don't feel rich until you hit the $30 million mark of investable assets. I know this may sound strange to some of you. Some of you may believe that the number is really $100 million, while others may believe that the number is really $5 million. However, if you ask all 7 million millionaires in America, $30 million in investable assets is the most common answer.

A business owner with between $2 million and $20 million dollars of investable assets is what I call the middle class millionaire. I want my potential client to be friendly, because I do this because I want to, not because I have to. Life is too short to deal with someone unfriendly. We are in the relationship business after all. The only thing we have to sell is trust. I also want potential clients to be serious about their money. I should not care more about your money than you do. There is an accountant I was working with. He was a named partner of an accounting firm, and he was not serious about his money. He said to me, "If I'm 80 and drooling and I'm out of money, I don't care." I care more about your money than you do? We're not a good fit. Sorry.

We also want our ideal client to be responsible. The CEO of a publicly traded company with a very large $45 million dollar portfolio sat down with me and he said, "I want to make a 15% return. In fact, I've got all my money right now in private equity." It didn't matter that after taxes his 15% return was closer to about 8%. It didn't matter to him that he was locked up and illiquid. I just don't feel that was responsible. We declined to take him on as a client.

Focus on getting better clients. How do you do this? Well, it's hard work. You've got to get your hands dirty. That's what we do. We can help you with that. There are systems for it. There are systems for success. Many of you have read my **bestselling book,** *The Power Principles of Success.* Everything is a system. Use them to attract a better client, not more prospects.

And in keeping with the language of trust, I encourage you to eliminate the word "prospect" from your vocabulary, when what you really mean is "potential client," or "opportunity for a new relationship." Prospect is demeaning to the potential client and to us as a profession.

Chapter 3
Generational Marketing

Generational marketing is the concept that, because of the impending massive transfer of wealth between generations, by marketing to the succeeding generation (G2 and G3), you will be able to gain them as clients.

Generational Marketing is a waste. The reason generational marketing is a waste is because you are told that there is about $13 trillion worth of generational wealth transfer that's likely to occur in the next several years as the seniors and boomers (G1) begin to die off. And the marketing gurus who do not have their own financial services business are telling you that if you would only develop relationships with the next generation of G2 and G3 that you'll be able to retain your assets as G1 begins to die off.

We are all concerned with the self-liquidating asset pool, where our clients are no longer accumulating, but distributing. And as they distribute, they require more of a service model. This makes it even more difficult to replace that depleting asset, due to resource constraints in providing that extra service and keeping your back door closed. And as they deplete, there's less to go around even to generation two and generation three. So it clearly would make sense to try to retain G2 and G3. Except, it doesn't work. And here's why it doesn't work.

You have to figure that about 10% of a client's assets, what's left after depletion due to distributions, is going to tax and other expenses. So that leaves 90%. And, typically, there are three beneficiaries. Often it's divided up into one-third each.

So, of the remaining 90%, roughly one-third of the beneficiaries have another advisor somewhere else. They already have a relationship, they're doing fine, and they're just going to want to move that money to that other relationship. Another 30% or one-third of the beneficiaries will not be good stewards of the assets. They are not very good at saving and accumulating and they're going to be spending that money right away. So only about one-third or 30% of that asset will you have a chance to retain.

Ask yourself this: how much effort should you put in to only 30% of the asset? And, yes, we agree. It is certainly less costly, and fewer resources are required to retain an asset than to acquire a new asset. However, for only a 30% hit rate, it might be worth your time to seek new replacement, and preferably *accumulation* assets. That is what this book is all about.

Make great decisions.

Chapter 4
Opportunity Abounds

There is an abundance of opportunity. How do you attract more opportunity? In order to attract more opportunity you have to get your head out of the computer. It doesn't make a lot of sense for you to be spending all of your time doing money management, working on and worrying about the *back office*.

Adam Smith in the 1770s showed that "division of labor" is one of the keys to success. We can do it ourselves. We should not, because others may do it more efficiently and more effectively. And because *your best use of time is client relationship management*.

Adam Smith

Specialize. Generalists do not earn as much as specialists. Specialize in your client relationship. All else is a costly distraction.

So, in order to attract opportunity, and to specialize, begin buying back more time by taking advantage of third party portfolio management. Specialization is also a big part of Exclusivity. Most of you utilize a core-satellite investment approach. Now, we at Summit don't do satellite, tactical risk-on/risk-off. We are not attempting to "beat the markets". We are core strategic. If you are tactical, that is fine.

We use exclusively True Market™ Models unified accounts managed for our clients' core, strategic investments. They specialize in that. Full disclosure: I am the CEO of the registered investment advisor that sponsors them. And all my own family investments are in these models.

True Market™ Models' portfolios are multi-asset class global ETF active strategic indexing funds. They have beaten the blended benchmarks by 1-2% every year for the past 12 years. You can access them on your overlay manager's platform provided by your custodian. They do it inexpensively. They do it effectively. They've got powerful performance.

It has made our lives so much easier since we went that route. It has made our clients so much stickier and more willing to make referrals. And by the way, we don't even ask for referrals. Why would I want to do that to my clients? They don't like that. It puts them in an uncomfortable position.

You simply want to give yourself more time. More time to develop, and better client relationships. Period. Another way to have more time is to "weed your garden." If you've got high demand clients who are not profitable, who are not fun, have someone else take care of them. If you feel an obligation you can still have someone else in your organization help you take care of them. But do the things that your clients perceive as the most valuable to them.

As Zig Zigler said, "You can get anything you want if you help others get what they want." Give your clients what they want and you can have what you want. That will help you attract more opportunity. It makes you more attractive to the referring centers of influence. We can show you how to make this happen.

What are the sources of alpha? The sources are lower expenses and a disciplined approach to buying low and selling high. It's pretty basic. That's how we deliver our *Alpha*. Contact my office to get my book ***The Science of Successful Investing.***

What about *Gamma*?

What is gamma? Gamma is the extra value your client receives for the money they pay you. Do you know how many clients want to know how much money you are making from providing them service. Why not be transparent? Transparency is part of the language of trust. Tell them exactly what the commission will be in a commissionable product. Tell them exactly what the fee will be. Tell them exactly what the risks are, what the benefits are, and what the alternatives are.

It's the same language I used when getting consent for surgery. What the risks, the benefits, the alternatives and the likely outcomes are. I told everybody who was going to have a cataract or Lasik surgery that they could go blind or lose their eye from the procedure. In fact, I would tell them that there was a 1 in 30,000 chance they could die from the anesthesia.

I have done 20,000 surgical cases, and I have never had one person tell me that they were unwilling to do the eye surgery because of the risks. Likewise, not one client left our firm when the markets tanked in 2008. We attribute this in large part to the use of simple, solid, safe (I know, all investments involve risk), portfolio management transparency, accountability and the language of trust.

Also, you need to demonstrate to and quantify for your clients the gamma that you bring in your relationship. And make them aware of it. They want to know what you get out of it, and what they get of it. This is what they get out of it:

We will find you a more efficient portfolio. (Worth 0.5%)

We will make sure that your portfolio is periodically properly allocated. (Worth 0.5%)

We will bring you the service that you're looking for so you don't have to do all the paperwork and the dirty work. (Worth 0.5%)

We will help you in other aspects of your financial life (Worth 0.5%)

We will provide you with advice when you are making major financial decisions, that is, financial planning. (Worth 0.5%)

We will help you with behavioral investment counseling (Worth 3-7%, according to DALBAR).

Even if you cut these values by half or more, you can see the value. Take away the mystery of your value, and your clients will be proud to pay the price.

I think you all will agree that avoiding losses is more powerful than picking winners. I think you will also agree that avoiding the 10 worst days in the market is much more powerful than hitting the 10 best days in the market over a determined time period. Now, I don't know anyone smart enough to reliably,

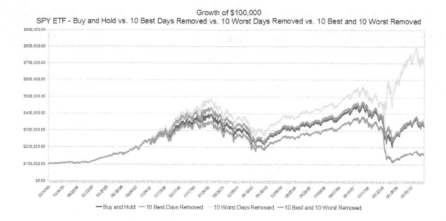

Growth of $100,000
SPY ETF - Buy and Hold vs. 10 Best Days Removed vs. 10 Worst Days Removed vs. 10 Best and 10 Worst Removed

— Buy and Hold — 10 Best Days Removed   10 Worst Days Removed — 10 Best and 10 Worst Removed

consistently, and predictably do both, or either for that matter. If you can find the person who can do both, fantastic. That's your satellite. That's your tactical approach. Go for it. We just want to be the core.

That's why we've implemented the True Market™ Models' strategic core portfolio investments. You should use them to develop your core investment portion of the portfolio. Their story is compelling. It is easy to understand and easy to explain, especially for those whose eyes glaze over talking numbers or those who don't really have an interest in finance.

It fits in well with the satellite and tactical components, too. They are efficient, transparent, accountable, and they have integrity. Not only that, they will supply you with tools to help you grow, cut costs, and have more time. Those are our sources of alpha and how we deliver gamma.

Chapter 5
Tell Me, and Show Me You Love Me

Do your best clients know that they are your best clients? How do you tell them? How do you show them? What are you doing to recognize them? What percentage of their business do you currently own? How many of their peers do you have as clients?

Make a point of demonstrating to them that you appreciate their business. You can schedule events like a trip to the symphony or a cruise. You can buy them a case of wine or hire a private chef at your office or a dessert tasting. It doesn't have to be expensive. Even a multimillionaire still appreciates free stuff. People want to know that they're getting something extra. They want recognition. Give 'em what they want.

You don't have to make this appreciation event a marketing event. In fact, I recommend you have two types.

One is *exclusively* for your best clients. Let them know it is exclusive for them and them alone. Not for marketing. They will appreciate it, and it will strengthen your relationships. These can be intimate affairs. And they can be larger. The possibilities are endless.

The other *is* for meeting new opportunities. Let your clients know that, too. There is no reason to be embarrassed about it, or to hide it. At first, you will have only clients. Eventually, one or two may bring an appropriate guest. Ultimately, many will bring appropriate guests. Recognize and reward your clients for bringing guests, in front of the guests.

Event Marketing

These can be as intimate as a couples dinner, or a little larger if you bring in an expert speaker, or a local celebrity. Find out what your ideal clients want, and give it to them. Most do not want it to be a networking event, so keep it to fewer than 25 people total. Small events can deliver big returns. Educate and more importantly entertain. Do not focus on financial issues. Be creative and make it fun for you and your clients and their guests.

Try a dessert tasting, a cigar tasting, a scotch or wine tasting, a cooking class, a back yard barbecue, a fishing trip, exclusive art shows at your local museum, several tickets to the opera or a sporting event. We hosted, "Diamonds and Engines", at a vintage exotic automobile garage, where we also invited a jeweler and held a fashion show so that the women would enjoy themselves as well. Hire an outside event planner to help you.

Don't be "that guy". Be yourself, without being needy. They will get it. Let everyone know how much you appreciate them, and how much fun it is to do business with you. You will be amazed how rapidly and inexpensively your practice will grow. It is a misunderstood and under-utilized practice-builder. Be creative. Enjoy your clients, your business and your growth.

Regarding gifts, a gift is not an unpaid advertisement you give your clients and potential clients. Avoid using your logos on gifts. Your logos can go on your center of influence marketing pieces, not on your client appreciation gifts.

Chapter 6
The Worst Excuses For Not Listening to My Advice

"Mitch, we don't have the same practice." The first inclination that most financial advisors have when they first hear me speak or read one of my articles or books is that "This might work for you, but I have a different business. You don't understand, my clients/ community/ business/ are different from yours." This narrow-minded thinking is nothing but an excuse for you to stick to the beaten path. The marketing ideas contained in this book are working across the country. They work for other professional practices and for other businesses.

The reason they work is that people are similar. We are all programmed the same way and no matter what we are selling, consumers make decisions about what they will purchase and whom they will work with in a remarkably similar fashion. This is a controversial idea in the financial advisor business. "We are different." But how? And how do you demonstrate that difference? Certainly you should show up differently. We will continue to explore this topic throughout the book.

I have heard this statement numerous times throughout my careers. You have a choice. You can keep on doing what you've been doing if you are happy with the way things are. Or you can make a change. Successful entrepreneurs recognize that continuing to do what you have tried in the past and expecting a better result is insane.

Chapter 7
What Business Are You Really In?

Remember when I asked you to write down three reasons why your clients should do business with you, and you could not use the words "quality," "service," or "we care?" It seems that all businesses claim these words. Everyone expects quality, service and care, so much so that it has become a commodity. You need a Unique Value Proposition (UVP).

Our friendly regulators have made it much more difficult to differentiate ourselves and tell people what makes us different. Summit Wealth Partners, Inc.'s UVP is "Solid Growth. Safely Managed. Trusted Advice™". We are in the trust/relationship business. Our widget is wealth management.

What is your UVP? If you would like help developing it, send me an email at MLevin@MySummitWealth.com including the 1, 2, or 3 reasons why clients should engage you.

Now, to answer what business you really are in: **you are in the business of growing and marketing your products and services**

through relationships. Period. Trust is the only thing you have to sell. All of our products and services are the same. Or at least they are perceived to be the same. From pizza, to law, to software, to financial services, the only difference is the widget and the type of relationship.

So focus on growing your business. Otherwise, be satisfied with what some describe as a lifestyle business. It is ok. It is what most dentists and surgeons have. For those of us who truly are building a business, remember the phrase, "You are either green and growing or ripe and rotting." What is the first step to grow your business? Work *on* your business more than you work *at* your business.

Financial advisors who are recognized as being the best spend no time on back office services and virtually no time on investment portfolio management. They outsource their back office functions. Call our office at 407-656-2252 and we will give you some resources for back office functions that are highly cost effective. More importantly, the most successful financial advisors use third party money managers. Spend more time with your clients and prospective clients than in front of your Bloomberg monitor.

If you have some extra portfolio expertise, you probably only use it in the tactical satellite portion of the portfolio anyway. The core portion (50—80%) of the portfolio should be outsourced. A great resource is True Market™ Models CORE portfolios (www.TrueMarketModels.com). They are available through your custodian's relationship with "overlay" managers like PlaceMark, Envestnet, Asset Mark, and others. This will lower your clients' costs and lower your clients' taxes. It will also improve your clients' diversification, allocation, and repositioning. Let your clients know that. They will appreciate it, and it will make them "stickier."

Chapter 8
The Elevator Speech.

Let's look at the "elevator speech." When someone asks what you do, how do you answer? Do they smell "sales breath"? Is your answer positioning you away from the language of trust?

Too many sales and marketing "experts" recommend you do just that. As you can already tell, I believe you must show up differently. So how do you answer? How should you answer? What are the gurus suggesting? You have probably heard something like, "I am in the business of doing XXXXX for people just like you," or "Do you know how some people struggle with XXXXX, well I help them do better." Someone else asks, "Are there some things you would like to fix in your investments? That is what I do". Watch out, he is going to sell me. He does not care about me.

Someone says, "I help people access their retirement funds at any time for any reason and tax free". He sells cash value life insurance. Or "I help people be certain that they will never run out of money and never lose money in market downturns". He sells annuities. Or "I help people find money they did not know they were losing". She sells financial planning.

How about this? When I was an eye surgeon, I told people that I was an eye surgeon. Now I say, "I run a wealth management firm that I believe is completely different from the others." Either someone asks you for more information, or they are not interested. End of story. Keep it simple, authentic, and not about you. What is different is that we believe and engage in comprehensive, collaborative planning and use or offer every financial tool available to put the client in a better position.

Chapter 9
Networking

"Networking." I am not a fan of this word. I would rather see it called "relationship exploration." Because that is what it is. How many times have you gone to a networking event to buy something? Never; and neither has anyone else, so stop trying to sell at these events. Leave your business cards at home.

Since every one else brings a card, show up differently and leave yours at home. Ask others for theirs. Spend time looking at it. Ask questions about the information on their card. It helps show that you care about people, and it puts you in control of future communications. Ask permission to communicate with them. Then when you get back to the office, write them an email to show how trustworthy you are by saying, "as promised, here is my communication…" We have a separate course on this topic. Call my office to see how you can access it.

When you are at a cocktail party, and you meet a cardiac surgeon and ask what he does, does he answer "I help people like you have the comfort and peace of mind to know their heart will never give out on them"? Of course not. First, snooze. Second, sales breathe. Third, unprofessional. Refer to the chapter on the elevator speech.

So why do these sales and marketing gurus, who have never been a successful financial advisor, advise you to speak like that? Would it not be better to use the language of trust?

Why not just say, as in my case, "I run a wealth management firm that focuses on collaborative comprehensive planning." Simple and true. No script to memorize.

Or you could say, "I am a financial advisor who caters to small business owners"; or "I am a wealth advisor who specializes in retirees"; or any thing else that is short, sweet and genuine. No sales breath. Professional.

If they are interested, they will ask you more. If not, do not offer. If *Glen Gary, Glen Ross* suggested that you "always be closing," I suggest you only be opening. In these understandably untrusting times, people have their radar on high alert. Most sales are lost in the opening, not the closing.

Use the language of trust. Act and speak in a trustworthy manner.

In a networking event, your job is to develop relationships. That is all. You want to develop new ones and reinforce existing ones. Then you can figure out if there is an opportunity to help each other. That may turn into business, but not necessarily, and that's fine.

To be really good at networking, play the host. Do not eat, and definitely do not drink alcohol. This is work. Ask people whom they would like to meet, what their business does, who their ideal client is and why someone would do business with them. Find someone meaningful to introduce to them. If they ask you some good questions, you may have an opportunity for a new relationship. If not, you have done your good deed and it is time to move on.

And not every after-network relationship is going to be fruitful. Fewer still result in a business relationship. That is fine too. Your job is to build relationships. That is not only your primary job, it is the only job that pays you. Every thing else, *every thing else*, is a cost center. Outsource it.

Outsource HR, compliance, money management, reporting, billing, planning—everything that does not put you in front of a meaningful or potentially meaningful relationship.

Chapter 10
Prospecting and COI Marketing

You must always be filling the funnel with potential clients. After all, as a successful, high integrity, respected professional, you want to help others. It matters not how good you are if you are not helping others. So you must always be searching for ways to identify and develop new client relationships.

You already know that I do not like calling people "prospects". This is worth repeating in keeping with the language of trust. It could be inferred as demeaning. They are potential clients, potential relationships, or potential opportunities to help. But not "prospects". Nevertheless, there is no better description for identifying new potential relationships than "prospecting".

Prospecting is so important, that it almost requires its own book. We will only briefly discuss it here. This is doing what others will not. It is our equivalent of manual labor, getting your hands dirty. This does not mean cold calling.

First, identify your ideal client. Please do not say anyone with large enough assets for you to manage. Think about the automobile industry. KIA™ and Lexus™ are both excellent cars. They sell to different types of people. Their UVPs are different. So their message should also be different. ***The message must match the medium and the market.***

KIA™ says "We wanna see ya in a KIA". Lexus™ says, "The relentless pursuit of perfection." These are very different messages for very different markets.

You need to figure out where your ideal clients hang out. Go there. Determine what they want. Then give that to them. Free. That does not mean working for free. That entails too much liability. Make yourself a trusted and reliable resource. Good things will happen, I promise.

Prospecting is difficult and not always immediately rewarding. If you are willing to do it, you will be successful. There is no magic, no secret to success other than a willingness to <u>do what others will not</u>. For more on that, see my best-seller, ***"The Power Principles of Success"***.

Prospecting means developing as many high quality relationships as you comfortably can, while being certain to maintain the highest quality relationships with your existing clients. While you can do this virtually anywhere, you should not. Be judicious. Your daughter's wedding is not the place to prospect.

Centers of Influence (COIs) are not restricted to accountants and attorneys. They also include business brokers, real estate agents both residential and commercial, mortgage brokers, business consultants, others in peripheral financial services such as property and casualty insurance, and so many more. <u>Here is the formula to get them to refer</u>: Help the COIs get more clients themselves. Simple, right? But not so easy.

Attorneys and accountants seem to hold the keys to good client referrals. And it is not about the money. So don't go there. It would position you as a notch below a used car salesman. Attorneys and accountants hold themselves as the clients' professional advocates. If they want to share in revenue, they will ask. Always position yourself as the consummate trusted professional.

In the case of CPAs and JDs, they have very little upside to refer, and much downside. You might not be so competent. You might mess up the relationship. You might recommend something they do not agree with, or may interfere with what they are trying to accomplish. You might be perceived as a threat. You might be perceived as a complicating factor in their ability to get new clients. After all, we provide them most of their clients. So they want to have as many sources of "us" as they can.

To help them get more clients is very complicated because you do not have enough clients who need their services, and the old "you refer to me-I refer to you" method just does not work. However, we have an extensive module in our exclusive *Winners' Core*™ master-mind group in which we go into it in detail. It is a long, slow process of relationship marketing. The success rate is exceedingly high and well worth it. Contact me directly for details as to your eligibility for the Winners' Core™.

Not only are these understandably untrusting times, this is one of the most difficult times to be in business. Any business. This is perhaps the most difficult time to develop our business than any other time prior. The economy as of this writing is horrendous. Regulations seem over-powering. Despite all of the adversity, some of us are growing. You can too. Be better. Do better.

Enough said.

Chapter 11
How Top, Successful Financial Advisors Think and Behave

Whether or not you become a successful advisor does not hinge on where you went to school or where you were born. Many top advisors did not attend what would be considered the best colleges, and some never even went. However, they typically share some basic characteristics.

People tend to learn things in one of two ways. Some learn through trial and error. They try, they fail, and then they take an action to correct their mistake and try again. This process can be very time consuming. Successful entrepreneurs generally use a second method. They look to see what successful people are doing around them, and they take those behaviors and ideas and adopt them for their own use. They are using other people's experience to help better themselves.

Take some time and reflect. What type of person are you really? You can be exposed to great ideas on a daily basis and never truly grasp them unless you think and behave like an entrepreneur. You do not need to have extensive experience running other businesses in order to be a successful financial advisor, but you should think of yourself as more than just a financial advisor. You are a business owner and an innovator.

What follows are some of the ways that successful financial advisors behave and think.

One Predictor of Success is Whom You Keep Company With– Whom do you associate with on a daily basis? Do you associate with people who uplift you, or do you hang out with people who whine and bring you down? If you want to earn more money, then you should be hanging out with people who earn more money than you do. They obviously know something that you do not. Always strive to associate with people who are going to bring your game up, not the other way around. You are the average of the 5 people you spend the most time with. (Forgive me for ending the sentence in a preposition).

It is OK to Profit – You should feel good about your work, and strive to make your business as profitable as you possibly can. Working as a financial advisor is great because you get to help people on a daily basis, but the truth is that you cannot properly help people unless you are making money. If all your thoughts are about how you are going to make your next payroll, there is no way for you to properly focus on your clients and their needs.

Are you more stressed when a lot of money is flowing into the business, or when no money is flowing in? In order to be operating at your best, which means the best service for your clients, you need to be making a profit. The financial advisor, whose business runs as a well-oiled marketing machine that constantly brings a stream of new clients in the door, is a better financial advisor to those clients.

Time Management: Be Extra Protective of Your Time – You need to be stingy with your time. Many of us feel like we are going full speed at all hours. Time is irreplaceable, yet it seems like so many people treat it like an unimportant asset. It is important that you appreciate the value of your time and the contributions that you bring to the world.

Every thing that can be done more efficiently by others should be delegated. See Chapter 4 regarding third party portfolio management, and back office functions. Time management is too detailed to develop for this book. I have another complete module on time management. Contact me to obtain.

You Need To Have An Abundance Mentality- Great entrepreneurs share the mentality that it is a big world out there and there are endless opportunities. Believe this, and your whole outlook on the ideas that you come across will change. Financial advisors who are exposed to various innovative ideas, yet remain stuck in mediocrity, do so because they have a scarcity mentality. They are of the belief that there is not enough to go around. Not only do they not share what they know with others, but they also shun the ideas of others as well. This is a terrible way to approach life.

You Alone Are Responsible For Your Financial Failure and Your Success- Do not be tempted to blame others for your own lack of success. Successful entrepreneurs do not make excuses for themselves. They realize that it is not an ideal world that we live in, and that it is one's own responsibility to seek the best for their client.

Don't fall into the trap of self-sorrow and pity. Always remember that there are financial advisors in every area of the country that are finding massive success. Successful entrepreneurs know that for every colossal business like Target, there is a mom and pop store that is thriving. Great business owners take responsibility for their own prosperity and seek out those more successful than themselves, and ask them how they achieved what they did. Finding success is more about your own choices than it is the actions of others.

Don't Be Afraid To Go Against Conventional Wisdom- If you are new to an industry, and do not know how you should go about being successful, a great piece of advice would be to observe what everyone else is doing in that industry and do the opposite. You want to model yourself on what successful people are doing. However, if you are unable to identify who the successful people are, the best advice is to observe what the pack is doing, and then do the opposite. Copy what everyone else is doing, and you will be undifferentiated and average. There will be no compelling reason for prospective clients to seek you out.

For example, if you wanted to run an ad in a magazine, you should look to see what other financial advisor's magazine advertisements look like. You will probably notice that all of the ads that you find are very similar to each other. Do you really want an advertisement that looks exactly like every other financial advisor's? The answer is, of course not. However, this is what advertisement sales representatives want to sell you. You are not setting yourself apart, and you will be lucky if a prospective client just happens to choose you from the pack.

Do Not Be Afraid To Discriminate- If you have not already done so, you should take time to write down the profile of your perfect client. Once you have done that, you should be making the effort to only be marketing to those clients that meet that description.

What type of client do you love working with? What type of client brings in the most revenue? What type of client do you hate working with? Successful business owners realize that it is perfectly acceptable for them to have a perfect customer in mind, and then build a business that is designed around meeting the needs of that customer.

It is perfectly acceptable to treat the clients that you want differently than the clients that you do not. In addition to bringing you the clients that you want, your marketing should help push away the client that you do not want. The riches are in the niches.

You Are Not A Commodity- You are not the same as all the other financial advisors out there. If you believe that you are no different than the rest, than there is no way that you can rise above all the rest.

These are some of the ways that financial advisors can differentiate themselves from the pack.

Your unique differentiator is…..you. Tell your story. We can help.

Develop a unique answer to why a prospective client should hire you.

Find a niche to fill. You do not have to be a generalist.

Create and sell an experience.

Create, sell and deliver by a system.

Create a unique marketing system so that people come to recognize and associate you by your type of marketing.

Make Yourself Immune To Criticism- As you gain more success, you are going to draw more criticism. That is just a fact of life. People will be jealous of your success, and upset with the fact that you are doing something different than everybody else.

Do not listen to them. Very few people are in position to cast judgment upon you or your marketing tactics. The only person responsible for your success is you. The naysayers are not the ones who are responsible for running your practice. As long as you are running an ethical marketing campaign that you are proud of, then there is no reason for you to listen to the voices of your critics.

Chapter 12
There Is A Blueprint For Success

It is absolutely true that successful people act in similar ways. (See my national bestseller, "The Power Secrets of Success".) They also leave blueprints for success, which you are free to follow. Most successful people have several things in common.

First, successful people tend to have a clear idea as to where they are going. They have clearly defined and actionable goals. One of the best things that you can do is to write down your goals. It is not enough to have your goals floating around in your head. Actually write them down. It is helpful to write them in pencil, so you can update them as need be. Keep your list of goals close by and read them frequently in order to remain motivated.

Second, successful people associate with other successful people. If you surround yourself with whiners and losers they will drag you down to their level. The opposite is also true. If you hang around positive, goal-oriented people, they will motivate you to be the best person that you can be. If you start associating with people who are more successful than you, you will be able to copy their blueprint for success and will be on track to accomplishing your own goals and dreams.

Third, successful people are constantly improving themselves through mastermind groups, study groups, the use of books, audio recordings and other media. Most successful people have a voracious appetite for new ideas. They are always consuming new information and looking for ways to improve themselves. Gradually, they begin to increase the pace at which they learn. They do not waste time on trivial things or unproductive acts.

There is a blueprint for success. Ask yourself every day, how many people am I helping today? You should get in the habit of learning something new every day and associating with other positive, successful people. Write down your goals so that you know what you really need to focus on, and leave the rest by the wayside. Make sure that you have clearly defined what success means for you.

PART II
TAKE ACTION

Begin at the beginning. There is a big difference between selling and marketing, though they are related. Be consistent in the language of trust. Speed helps.

Chapter 13
The Broad View

In this chapter I am going to give you an overview on "outbound" or "outreach" marketing your practice. You should consult this list often as you decide how to expend your precious time and hard earned dollars on marketing your financial advisory business.

Accept that clear and effective marketing is complicated. There is no easy path here.

Only you have the power to decide who you want to come to your business as your next client.

It is imperative to have an automated database for marketing purposes.

Develop and grow your fan base and your herd.

Touch base with your fans 12-28 times a year, primarily by mailing them an interesting and well-produced newsletter. Emailed newsletters are no substitute for hard copy.

Continually refine and perfect your inbound media. Clients will be looking for you on the Internet as well as other centers of influence.

Understand and maximize client's ability to find your webpage through search engine optimization.

Grab attention with bold headlines and powerful copy.

Make an offer that grabs the attention of prospective clients and gets them to ask for more information.

Deliver information and advice to your clients that will convince them that you are the preeminent expert in your field.

Continually and constantly follow up.

Continue to grow your client base.

Have a reason for them to contact you.

Do not forget the call to action that eliminates threshold resistance.

Chapter 14
Financial Advisor Marketing is Complex

You have to remember that there is no one thing that you can do to get more clients. Bringing in new clients is complex and it is not easy. It requires doing many things right. You cannot just tweak an advertisement and expect to see a parade of prospective clients rushing through your door.

You work in a highly competitive field. There are countless financial advisors out there who all look the same to a prospective client. It is hard for potential clients to know whom to turn to for advice.

Most financial advisors want a simple solution to this very complex problem. They will run additional ads that get lost among the sea of other financial advisor's ads, or they will pump money into the design of a website that ends up looking like every other advisors website. You have to remember that there is no simple answer to this very complex problem, only complex answers.

A complex multi-step media marketing system can serve to:

Differentiate your business from financial advisors who use the traditional marketing approach of buying an advertisement and offering a free consultation;

Establish you as the go to financial advisor for complex issues without your having to say so;

Keep away potential clients outside of your target demographic. While this may "feel" wrong, it is impossible to provide great service to all, or to just about anybody;

Increase the transaction value of each client, thus freeing you up to spend more time doing the things you love to do, while making more money.

Here are some of the typical objections that we receive to implementing such as system.

If I do not speak with the client immediately, they will go to another financial advisor.

Potential clients do not want to read so much material.

I need to take on all clients, no matter what the size.

Small clients do not take up that much time, and they help pay the bills.

Your plan is too expensive.

I only go to you for your money management skills

Do not listen to these objections.

It Is Not Necessary For You To Deliver An Immediate Response- You do not ever want to be viewed as a commodity. Nor do you have to become a financial butler. Do not get in the habit of letting potential clients think that if they do not select you, the next financial advisor they find is a suitable replacement. Who else but you will do a better job? You are after all, a trusted professional adviser. They need you more than you need them. You want them, though, and you want them to succeed. And you want to deliver extra value with great care and *speed*, to be in alignment with the language of trust.

People will always have a fear of missing out. Financial Advisors think that unless they make themselves constantly available, they will miss out on potential clients. The truth of the matter is that you are already missing out on potential clients. There are other financial advisors in your area that you compete with, and there is no way for you to sign every single client in town. It is simply not possible.

Think about this. When you want a great steak, do you make plans to go to the best place in town where you need to make a reservation several weeks in advance, or do you just settle for the half empty restaurant around the block? People who are entrusting you with their retirement funds, their life's work want the best financial advisor that they can find, and they are willing to wait a little in order to ensure that they do. You do not need to sign a client the minute that they call. It is ok, and sometimes preferable to take time in developing a super strong relationship.

Clients *Are* Willing To Take The Time To Read The Material-
Potential clients unwilling to read the material that you send to them are unlikely to heed your advice anyway. While it is true that not every client you send promotional material to is likely to read every single word, the mere fact that you are taking the time to send them all that material makes you unique. A certain level of credibility is established by sending them all that information.

Preparing educational material also gives you a great reason to keep sending potential clients information. Continually sending information serves to reinforce your message. While your prospective client may choose to speak with other financial advisors, they will continue to receive information from you. Following up with a client can really be the deciding factor when hiring a financial advisor. Persistency, part of the language of trust, counts. Life gets in the way of client decision-making. Respect that and help them by being persistent.

Sending multiple packs of information also gives you a reason to follow up with a potential client. You can reach out to see if the client has watched or read your information, and whether or not they have any questions that you can answer. You do not have to be pushy here, just offer guidance and help. Your informational materials help to sell you without you having to be obnoxious about it.

You Do Not Need To Take Every Client That Comes Your Way- One reason for not accepting every client that approaches you is that it takes time away from focusing on the clients you really want to be helping. While you may choose not to take on a certain client at a particular time, it can still be helpful to continue to send them information. Just because an individual does not fall into your target demographic today, does not mean that they won't be in your target demographic tomorrow.

Small Clients Do Take Time- Have you ever tracked the time you spend on clients who are not your perfect client? I think that you would be surprised at how much time you spend with clients who might not actually be worth the effort. You do not have unlimited time, and is it not better to devote your resources to clients that offer the best rate of return. Some even believe that smaller clients are more likely to engage in complaints or litigation.

You also can build a great practice with smaller clients who are often underserved. Just adjust your service model to retain profitability, and help manage their expectations accordingly. You should aim to work smarter, not harder.

You can refer potential clients who do not meet your specifications to other financial advisors in your area. This will help the potential client and also allow you to build alliances with local financial advisors.

A Complex Marketing System Is Worth The Expense- It is not written in stone that a complex marketing system need be expensive, but then again it might be. Take time to consider the fact that a typical marketing system may be equally expensive and be much less effective in producing new clients. Plus, a typical marketing system will not help differentiate you from the pack of financial advisors already advertising. It is extremely difficult to build a marketing program without spending any money. You want to allocate your dollars in the most effective way possible.

Chapter 15
Your Herd

An extremely valuable asset for any financial advisor is the list that compiles the names and contact information of anyone who has expressed any interest in your firm whatsoever. They are the basis of relationship marketing. These are people who have granted you the permission to communicate with them.

They are your "herd", which I use as a term of endearment. This is in no way meant as denigrating. Other words with similar meaning you may be more comfortable with: flock, fan base, list, database, army, throng, pack, supporters, followers, disciples, devotees, and so many more. "A rose is a rose..." It does not matter which descriptor you use. As long as you identify and communicate with these people.

Your list should include the following:

Any person who has ever requested information from you or your business.

Every potential client from other sources who has contacted you.

Other financial advisors who are not competing for the same clients as you are.

All of your vendors.

All of your relatives and friends.

Other professionals (some call them Centers of Influence) who are in leadership positions in their own industry.

In order to keep track of potential clients you will need a software database that:

Automatically adds everyone who fills out a contact form on your website.

Is capable of importing contact information from your existing client management software.

Is able to tell you what specific piece of marketing a prospective client saw that made them to contact you.

Is easy enough to use that your staff will be able to add client information when first contact is made by phone.

Is capable of automatically responding to client inquiries in a personal way

Is able to sort prospects so that top referral sources can be identified and marketed to differently than other prospects on your list.

Chapter 16
To Whom Are You Marketing?

Do you have clients that monopolize your time and resources? Clients who seem like they are more trouble than they are worth? This problem can be traced to one source. You.

The problem is that you never defined what your ideal client would look like. You thought that in order to be successful you needed to serve anyone who came in the door, and as a consequence you never developed a vision of who your perfect client was.

Fortunately there is an answer, and that is also you. It is entirely possible for you to market to your perfect client. The clients that are not ideal for you may be perfect for somebody else, but as long as you are running your own financial advisory, I want you to market to the type of customer who is ideal for your business. It is not feasible for your advisory to take on every person who walks through your door on as a client.

It is important that you take time to define what your perfect client looks like. Once you have defined your client, take time to write down your vision. Now you will be able to create a marketing platform that speaks directly to your ideal client.

If one of the major problems in your business is that you are unhappy with the type of clients you are attracting, it is important to remember that your marketing attracted them, the fear that you needed to take on whatever business that walked through the door made you accept them, and that same fear prevents you from letting these clients go. Just remember, you can solve this problem by defining who your perfect client is, and marketing specifically to them.

Chapter 17
Communicating with your Herd
via Newsletter

We have already discussed some examples of the power of newsletters. Your newsletter exists to help you stay in the minds of your clients and to connect with your herd. Don't let it be boring. Your newsletter should be designed to recognize and reward your herd and to encourage introductions, without you asking directly.

There is no doubt that creating a compelling and interesting newsletter that can be mailed out each month is a lot of work. It is much easier to hire an advertising agency to shoot a commercial or design a yellow page ad that you can continue to use month after month.

The reality is that it is much more cost effective to have an existing client introduce you to new business than to obtain a new client on your own. In addition to telling the world who you are and what you are about, newsletters enable others to repeat your story to their friends and families.

Here is some advice that will enable you to produce a newsletter that people will want to read.

Do not send a newsletter if what you are sending is a canned newsletter produced by a third party. These newsletters are not engaging, do not speak to the specifics of your business, and more often than not, they are sent straight to the trash bin. If your newsletter reads exactly like the next financial advisor's newsletter, then you are not differentiating yourself and you would be wise to spend your money on something of more value. Canned newsletter providers do not know how to effectively market your financial advisory business.

Find a place to store interesting ideas that come to you throughout the month. It can be very daunting to look at blank piece of paper and realize that you have to write an entire newsletter from scratch. If you begin to store ideas, then you will have more than enough material to choose from when deciding what topics you want to write about in your newsletter.

Let your personality shine through in your newsletter. You have a unique life. You might not necessarily think that the details of your life are interesting, but other people will. Talk about your family and hobbies. Did you finish a marathon last weekend? Write about it. Let your readers know that you have a life outside your business and that you are a real human being.

If you write a blog, and there are very good reasons as to why you should, then you already have a source from which to create newsletter articles. Don't worry about reusing material. The more eyes that see it, the better.

If it makes you uncomfortable to write about yourself, then you should find someone in your community that you can write about. Is there another small business in the community that you find interesting? You can write about that business and when you publish the newsletter make sure to give that business copies that they can hand out. This will not only draw attention to a great local business, but also will raise your profile and bring the opportunity of possible referrals.

If you are pressed for time, you can always hire a ghostwriter. There are many good writers who would be able to come up with ideas they can turn into a newsletter for you. Just make sure that they are personalizing the newsletter to your business and not writing an impersonal newsletter that speaks to no one.

Don't be afraid to use photos of yourself or your family in the newsletter. People like to do business with people they like and trust. Using photos will help humanize you and make you more approachable in the eyes of your readers. They will be more likely to do business with you as a result.

Always be on the lookout for new ways to use an article. If you write an article for your newsletter, consider the possibility that the article can be repurposed for a website, blog, letter to the editor, or even for an article in the newspaper.

After you have written an article, be sure to submit it to Internet syndication sites. Syndication will spread your article throughout the Internet, and it will also give you a useful place to store the article. The article will be there for you whenever you want to pull it up, update it, and use it again.

If all else fails, we can help.

SUMMIT WEALTH
— PARTNERS —

Volume 4, Issue 18, June 2014

The Rational Optimist™

100 — How to Win in the Fourth Quarter
By Mitch Levin, MD, CWPP, CAPP
CEO and Managing Director

100 is a nice round number. Reading this may make you roll your eyes and smile, or you may wonder if I'm unrealistically super-optimistic. Age 100 could be the "new 75". 100 years ago, people were not expected to live to age 75. In fact, they were barely expected to live to age 65. Now it seems likely, many of us are going to live to age 100. Some feel biology will be to the 21st century what physics was to the 20th century.

Actuaries and insurance companies generally look backward not forward. They report past life expectancy, so don't be fooled by an expectancy age that presumes we won't get a cure for cancer. Don't accept a presumption that organ transplants won't become everyday operations. Don't expect we might not have a cure for many of our hereditary diseases. Taken all together, these medical advances are likely to *add a generation to our lives*. We have several genes isolated and involved in a treatment for Alzheimer's disease and over 22 drugs for it are in trial.

We have the first really good medication for schizophrenia and the FDA recently approved the first emergency drug that can protect against disability for someone having a stroke receiving it quickly enough. There may be treatments that will block the action of cocaine, and brain tissue transplants that will cure Parkinson's disease, and we'll be able to isolate more genes that cause manic depressive illness.

There are drugs available today that can induce injured spinal cord cells to reconnect. More of our wounded military are surviving injuries and able to maintain productivity in society. We may think of extreme old age as being a liability to society or a burden to family, falling apart physically and losing your marbles mentally. We may think of us in old age of making no contribution and worst of all of having no fun. Ask yourself, what if brain scientists are able to keep pace with the scientists of the body?

Since I was in medical school, and it doesn't seem so long ago, many so called non-curable cancers are now curable. AIDS, which was discovered while I was in medical school, has been effectively controlled, if not conquered. For young people today, it is suggested you throw out all previous notions of one career followed by a lazy retirement. That was the strategy of your grandfathers and is strictly "wheelchair thinking".

This past January, the Society of Actuaries (SOA) gathered in Orlando for their fifth triennial Living to 100 Symposium to address living longer and its global impact on work, society, retirement and

LIVING *to* 100
SOCIETY OF ACTUARIES
INTERNATIONAL SYMPOSIUM

health. When experts discussed the risks and advantages associated with living longer, it was noted that the biggest issues of concern for retirees included inflation, paying for healthcare and the risk of depleting their savings.

Anna Rappaport, chair of the SOA's Committee on Post-Retirement Needs and Risks, said "While a lot has been done to identify the related societal issues with living longer, relatively little work has been done to help people adapt to longer lives."

Continued on Page 6

What's Inside This Issue:

Chapter 18
Inbound Media.

When a prospective client decides that they need a financial advisor, they will generally take one of several actions. They may seek a referral from a friend or go to a financial advisor with whom they are personally acquainted. Or they may go looking for a financial advisor on the Internet or ask their COIs. They may respond to a seminar invitation, or direct mail, or a newspaper ad. They might call an advisor they heard on the radio or saw on TV. If the prospective client is consulting the Internet, "inbound media," then they will have numerous choices and many different firms vying for their attention. If you want to be competitive, then your website or other education and outreach efforts will need to:

Grab their attention

Get them interested in your message.

Have them start the conversation. You want the prospective client to request your free information package.

Pause their search for an alternative investment advisor while they take the time to listen to your marketing message. You can do this by including a "guide to hiring an investment advisor" which you can put in your information package.

Irrespective of the type of "inbound media," the structure should be the same.

A bold, attention grabbing headline.

Copy that will speak directly to your ideal client.

An offer that the prospective client will find irresistible.

Headlines- Make Sure That They Stick Around.

How do you decide what to read when you are skimming the newspaper? You read the headline. It is the headline that piques your interest and draws you in. The headline is what persuades you to read the rest of the article. For most financial advisors, the headline of their ad is predicable and repetitive. They are the same headlines that other financial advisors across the country are using. You have to ask yourself the question, why would any prospective client continue to read an ad with such an unremarkable headline? Instead of being predictable, differentiate yourself from other financial advisors by creating a bold and attention grabbing headline.

Copy

Many financial advisors begin their ad copy by speaking about themselves. This is a mistake. People in the market for a financial advisor do not typically ask themselves, "I wonder where Mitch Levin went to school and what associations he belongs to."

Instead, they are asking themselves about their own needs. Your ad would be much more effective if the reader, who should be your ideal client, felt that the ad was written just for them.

People are more interested in what you can do for them, then in what you do. Describe to them the benefit of working with you.

An Offer That The Prospective Client Will Find Irresistible.

Most ads placed by financial advisors have no call to action other than a line such as, "call us now for a free meeting," Or "come to my seminar." This is not compelling or attention grabbing. Besides, it creates too much "threshold resistance." You should strive to be different.

You can differentiate yourself from these "free meeting" ads by providing something of tangible value, such as an information resource. These information resources often take the form of a book or free report, and should be produced to answer questions that a typical prospective client may have. You want to create an information premium that the prospective client will feel the desire to request before they continue on their search for the right financial advisor.

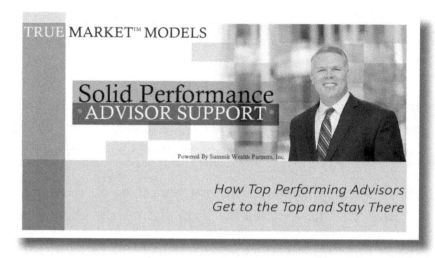

Being the advisor who literally "wrote the book," has added benefits. First, it incentivizes clients to identify themselves to you and begin a dialogue. Second, it establishes you as an expert in your field. The whole point of your offer is that you want to convince the prospective client that they need to request the information that you are offering before they make any decisions about which financial advisor to hire. Here is an example of one of our reports.

This special report is exclusively for successful financial advisors who want to achieve greater scalability in less time while earning a higher income.
— *this is for you.*

Do You Feel Like Most Financial Advisors . . .

Successful
Advisors
Leverage
Powerful
Partnerships

- As a sole practitioner, are you wearing too many hats?
- Do you wonder how others easily attract new client relationships?
- Are you spending too much time on portfolio management?
- Is marketing too time consuming and costly?
- Are assets under management not what you hoped?
- Is it harder to retain clients?
- Do you have too many held away assets?
- Is your compensation growing?
- Do you have a valid succession plan?
- Do you know how to maximize the value of your business and hard work?
- Are you concerned about giving up control and your independence?

Read this Report; We Can Help

Many advisors want and need answers to these questions. We have the answers. Read this report and discover how to differentiate and grow your firm. Your next greatest opportunity may be within your current client base without you even realizing it. Your worst threat to your success could be time management.

We will share with you how to devote more time to keeping your clients happy and confident by delivering meaningful, consistent results and how to enhance your relationships and communications with clients through simple marketing, while expanding your network of clients and growing your business effectively and efficiently. We have the answers.

Contact Us Today → 1-866-977-2252 → TrueMarketModels.com → UMAmarketplace.com/eisc

Having print ads and websites whose purpose is to make an irresistible offer have the additional benefit of not making your ad overbearing. Most advertisements by financial advisors try to make a sale immediately. They try to convince the prospective client that the financial advisor needs to be hired on the spot, all based on the one piece of marketing material the client viewed.

It is much easier to design an advertisement whose only purpose is to get the prospective client to request the book or report you are offering. What does your ad need to say in order to get people to request your book or report? Keep this question in mind when you are designing your next advertisement.

It is all well and good to get prospective clients interested in your book, but I'm sure that the question that is on all of your minds is when do I actually get to make a sale? The sale occurs, or at least is lost, at the opening. That is why it is important to show up differently. The sale occurs after that client comes to the conclusion, after your follow up marketing, that you are the best-qualified and most talented financial advisor out there who meets their needs.

Chapter 19
The Trick To Effective Follow Up

Be persistent. Life happens. Your prospective client may just not be ready. Do not give up until they tell you not to darken their doorstep. The challenge is to not become a pest. If you are serious about expanding the profitability of your business, then it is important that you consistently and effectively follow up with all of your prospective clients and clients.

You should be in a position of readiness for the moment when someone needs your services or a past client refers a prospective client to you. You also have to be on top of your game when a prospective client comes to your office for a meeting. So, why is it so important that you follow up with prospective clients? Why does it help differentiate you from the heap of other financial advisors out there? The reason is that people buy only when they are ready to buy. This often takes years. Be patient and gentle in your persistence.

Hiring a financial advisor is not an impulse buy. People do not seek out a financial advisor unless they are in need of one. But just because a person is not in the market for a financial advisor at this moment, does not mean that they will not need a financial advisor in the future.

If you have been following up consistently with all of your prospects, then you will be in a great position to turn a potential client into a client when that person is ready to hire a financial advisor. Here is why.

You Are Building Trust- The first time you consult with any prospective client, they will be sizing you up, making sure that you are a person that they feel comfortable conducting business with. You are doing the same, or should be.

If you keep in contact with potential clients you will start building a relationship with them. The longer the relationship, the more trust that you will build. They will begin to identify with you and be more willing to conduct business with you rather than some unknown advisor they have had no contact with. Once they are ready to hire a financial advisor, you will be the first one they will contact.

You Are Constantly Keeping Your Name In The Minds Of Potential Clients- Just because you are a great financial advisor does not mean that past and prospective clients are always thinking of you. Most people live busy lives filled with activities. A prospective client may have thought that your advertisement was great, but then just as easily forgotten about it.

It is likely that when a prospective client decides that they need a financial advisor, they are not thinking about you at all. Unless you constantly remind prospective clients of who you are, and why you are better than your competitors, prospective clients are likely to forget that you even exist.

If you consistently follow up with prospective clients, you are not giving them the opportunity to forget about you. If done properly, the minute a prospective client is in need of a financial advisor, they will think of you.

You Are Building Loyalty- Another great benefit of consistently following up is that it helps differentiate you from other financial advisors. This is because not a lot of financial advisors are following up with their clients and prospects. The reason for this is that they lose patience, they feel pressure to sell, and it is difficult to always follow up.

Even though it is not easy to consistently follow up, if you take the time to do it, you will see results. Clients and prospective clients will appreciate it. A major reason why clients do not give referrals is because they do not feel appreciated. You have the power to make them feel appreciated. Simply by following up, you can make a client or prospective client feel like they are your top priority.

What Happens When You Are Spread Thin?- You are no doubt a busy person. Running a financial advisory takes a lot of work, and you may find yourself stretched thin and wondering where you will find the time to follow up with your clients and prospective clients. A great way to handle this problem is to automate your business.

Automation works like this. A potential client is interested in hiring a financial advisor and so seeks out your website among others. On your website you have included a link to a free report that you have written that should be of interest to any prospective client in the market for a financial advisor. All the potential client has to do to access the free report is give their name, phone number and email address.

The prospective client is interested in the report, and so they give you the information that you ask for. Instead of manually entering the client's information, your automated system inputs the client's information into your database, and sends them the free report that they asked for.

If the client does not take immediate steps to contact you to set up an in-person meeting, then the automated system will be able to tell. It should be set up to follow up with the prospective client in the next few days in order to see if the prospective client has any questions. You can take this time to give the prospective client access to more information.

Using automation, you should be able to send prewritten, personalized letters, emails, faxes, postcards, and other pieces of marketing material to prospective clients at steady intervals. A prospective client may not be ready to hire a financial advisor for several years, but utilizing automated follow-ups, you will be at the forefront of that person's thoughts when they are ready.

You want to communicate as much as possible with prospective clients without becoming a nuisance. Using automation, you should be able to stay in contact with all of your current and prospective clients easily, and without adding more work to your busy schedule. This is a big reason why we recommend you delegate portfolio management and back office to third party experts.

PART III
LET'S GET "SPECIFICAL"?

We cannot afford brand building. We must get a direct quantifiable response from our efforts and we must measure our return on the marketing efforts.

Chapter 20
Introduction to the Inbound Marketing Media. The Internet.

For many financial advisors, the Internet is a hot topic and has become one of the primary ways to market their business. I personally know one advisor who brings in well over $700 Million (that is *not* a typo) per year of client assets -- through the internet. Others struggle. They lack a cohesive plan and have not taken the proper steps to maximize the Internet's potential as a marketing tool.

There is a common notion that websites and blogs are used to establish ones self as a thought leader. Prospective clients will then realize that you are the best in your field and will seek you out. At least that is the hope. This is just another example of the "do good work and they will come" mentality that so many financial advisors have. This is not the best strategy to market your business.

The purpose of your Internet marketing strategy should be to provoke prospective clients to initiate contact with you. Every thing that you post should make the prospective client drop what they are doing and think, "Before I go out and sign with any financial advisor, I absolutely need the free information that you are offering."

The Internet is like any other form of media. You don't have to change your message that much just because Internet is the media that you are using. It is important to promote yourself as an authority on your website, however if this is your primary strategy then you are sure to get beaten out by the competitor who is using the Internet as the tip of the sword of a comprehensive marketing campaign. The marketing gurus who stress that you need to be a thought leader and the business will just flow to you are wrong. It is essential that you get prospective customers interested enough that they are raising their hands and asking you for more information.

Your website must take the following steps in order to ensure that you have an effective web presence that draws prospective clients to contact you.

Make sure you are properly utilizing the search engine return page (SERP). This will ensure your widespread presence on the web.

Draw your audience in with a powerful headline. You can even make this a short video. Your name, logo, or a photo of your city is not a powerful headline.

Make sure that you have grabbed the potential client's interest long enough that they see the free information that you are offering. Get them to click on the link to submit contact information to you.

Transfer the contact information to your automated database and begin your multi-faceted sequence of marketing events.

How Any Financial Advisor Can Become The Master of Google

Becoming highly visible and maintaining that visibility on Google requires two things, technology and the willingness to work at it. It is no simple task to get your website on the first page of Google. Once you have achieved that goal though, it can be very hard for your competitors to knock you out of that position. The most talented financial advisor Internet marketers have been known to have more than one position on the front page of Google without their even having to buy Adwords.

The technology essentials that you will need:

1. A website content management tool. You no longer need to hire an expensive webmaster to make every miniscule change to your website. You should make sure that whoever maintains your website has set up a content management system that you have access to, in order that you can create and upload:

a. New pages

b. New content on already existing pages

c. Frequently asked questions

d. New practice areas

e. Images and photographs

f. Blog entries

g. News that pertains to your practice area

h. PDF documents

i. Video that can be automatically pushed to other video distribution websites.

j. Information request forms that automatically transfer contacts to your contact database.

If you have not set up a content management system that enables you to make these changes then you are already at a disadvantage. Google is always changing the way it perceives and ranks the utility of websites, but it is always true that new content is number one. Many financial advisors are hiring teams of writers to constantly create content for the Internet. Financial advisors who employ this strategy consider themselves publishers and the websites they run are media machines.

Does this sound like it is too much work? Well, you have a choice. You can stick with the strategy that you have been pursuing. This is certainly easier, but do not complain when your site is not producing the type of leads that you hoped it would. Or you can make a change.

2. Invest in software that tracks the terms that prospective client are using to come to your site. Google Analytics is a free tool that you should be using. If your web designer has not shown you how to utilize this useful tool then it is time for you to find a new web designer. This is important and could save you quite a bit of money. Plenty of financial advisors are willing to bid on vanity keywords such as "Florida financial advisor," but over 70% of searches do not use any vanity keywords. The typical prospective client will search in the form of a question or an extended phrase. It is important for your overall marketing strategy for you to know what the keywords are that are being used to find your business. This will enable you to create more content that is geared toward those long tailed keywords and make your business more visible on Google.

Chapter 21
What Your Internet Strategy
Should Not Consist Of

After you have installed your technology, then it is time to implement your strategy. The whole point of the website is to have the prospective client click on the button that requests additional information from you. With this in mind, let us examine some of the ways in which financial advisors make mistakes with their websites.

Having the top third of your main page be something generic such as your firms logo, the firms name, or a picture of yourself. This strategy does nothing to differentiate you from the rest of the herd. Always remember: you want to be different. When a potential client goes to your website you need to grab their attention in the first few seconds, lest they move on to a more interesting page. Some of the most successful sites use a video as part of their "headline"

Writing too much about you. Prospective clients do not look at a financial advisor's website because they are interested in where that advisor went to school or how long that advisor has been in business. They look at the website because they have problems that need solving. Your headline and copy must speak to these problems. You know what your client's questions and concerns are. Your copy must answer these questions and concerns. It is a waste of time for your first page to tell the client how much money you have under management. They do not care.

Forgetting to have compelling copy and headlines on all of the pages that make up your website. Consumers may not always come to your main page first. Every page that you publish must be created with the principles we have discussed in mind. You have to make sure that if a prospective client lands on any one of your pages, you can keep their interest long enough to convince them to click on a request for information.

Having a "contact us" link as the only way for a prospective client to initiate contact with you. You need to have a link offering some form of free product, a "freemium" and preferably a "bonus" too. Yes these are shameless and legal incentives. Financial advisors who use this strategy to launch a multistep, multimedia marketing campaign bring in more clients on a consistent basis.

Not having a "Live Chat" option on your website. Many websites have incorporated this option as another way to open a dialogue with potential clients.

Not taking the time to optimize your website for the search engine. In addition to knowing what a key word is, you should be familiar with the words title tag and meta description. Every page in your website should have a unique title tag and meta description that is focused on the key words you are optimizing that page for.

Chapter 22
Blogging Is A Form Of Social Media

Blogs- When composing blog entries make sure you keep the following in mind. You want to write often, write relevant, and make sure that your writing includes key words.

What does a good blog contain?

First, always keep in mind the audience that you are writing for. Do not write about a young man's problem if you are trying to target an older audience. Write to the wrong audience, and nobody will be listening.

Second, keep your writing simple and direct. Most people will zone out if your posts contain more than 300 words. This is the equivalent of a 3-minute monologue. Make sure to video record it.

People read blogs because they want clear and quick answers. There are other avenues available to them if they want a more in-depth analysis. So always keep your posts short and concise. Do this, and you will become a go-to source.

Third, make sure that you write actionable content. Actionable content includes lists, best practices, and how-to's. These are great because they give prospective clients ideas that they can utilize in their daily lives.

Fourth, do not be afraid to share some of your private knowledge with potential clients. People are always interested in hearing how something is done, even if they are not always interested in doing it themselves. If you share some information with potential clients they are unlikely to go out and become financial advisors. What is more likely is that they go out and hire you.

Fifth, make sure that your blog has a comment section. As the author, you should be the first one to post a comment after every blog entry. You can ask a question or post a comment to facilitate discussion. The more comments being written the better, because relevant content is being added which will be recognized and treated positively by the search engines.

If at all possible, you will want to syndicate your blog posts. This means that your posts will appear on thousands of sites throughout the web and will all link back to your original post. This will give your site a vote in Google for relevance which will allow it to climb higher in rankings, give you another listing in the rankings for the subject people searched for, and will also build your reputation as an expert among people who read your posts.

Blogging began as an effort to add new content to a website before decent content management systems existed. Today blogs are ubiquitous and there are many free resources that you can use to set up your blog.

You should not consider a blog to be a substitute for a well designed and robust website, but a blog is certainly a great additional tool to have in your arsenal. You should first create a great website for your financial advisory business. After you have done this, then you can go out and create blogs which will act to help you maintain dominance on the main page of Google, and act as feeders to your main website.

Blogs can be very helpful because a content management system is typically built into the blog engine. So once the blog is online it is relatively easy to add new content. The purpose of the blog should be to have potential clients identify themselves to you.

The best-designed blogs are set to create a traffic flow that is faster than websites, so it is important to keep in mind the way that search engines work when you are creating your blog. Here are some best practices to keep in mind when setting up your blog.

A Word on Compliance-Caution. Do not edit comments. The regulators will not be happy. Do not re-organize comments. The regulators will not be happy. This goes for all social media. Comments may be deemed a form of endorsement or testimonial if you "cherry pick." You must include the bad with the good and you should keep these in the actual sequence of delivery. Don't forget proper disclaimers and disclosures. You must have obtained permission to email and at the very least include your hard address, your name as the sender, an unsubscribe opportunity associated with electronic communications (see the CAN-Spam rules). This is not legal advice.

Structuring of Content- The software that you are using should enable you to categorize what you are blogging about. So if you are blogging about one area of your business, you should have a category to put it into. The software that you are using should allow you to create categories as you go along.

Easy to use URL's- The URL plays an important role in how a search engine finds what the user is looking for. In picking an appropriate URL, you should focus on simplicity. Choose a term that is directly related to what you are blogging about. Each individual topic that you are blogging about should have its own distinct URL. You want your blogging software to allow you to choose your own URL for that blog and not just randomly assign you a URL that has nothing to do with your topic.

Easy Internal Linking- Placing links to other parts of your website is a highly effective way for generating search engine traffic. If you write a blog article that references something that you have on your website, go ahead and create a link to that page. With most blog software it is as easy as cutting and pasting.

New Content- Search engines reward fresh content. Blogs are a great way for you to constantly be updating your site and give the search engines new material.

Active Feedback- Since blogs typically have the option to leave a comment; it is possible for the audience to give you immediate feedback. Comments can also be used to drive traffic to your websites. Comments offer the opportunity to load more text with key words and key phrases, and the great things is that you don't even have to write it.

Blogging Strategies

Peruse the newspapers for topics to write about.

Post the article you write about today's news on your main website.

Use your blogs to funnel readers to your article. The headline of your blog post should draw people in to look at your blog. Your blog then has a link that drives viewers back to your main website.

Get your readers involved. Ask them what they think.

Get into the habit of viewing everything as potential website or blog articles. There is a lot of good material out there.

Chapter 23
Using Online Video In Your Marketing Effort

In recent years there has been a real trend of financial advisors using online videos to establish their presence on the web. Potential clients like videos because they allow the client to get to know the financial advisor before speaking with them. Videos also allow the potential client to asses whether they like you or not.

Financial advisors who are not utilizing online videos in their practice are losing out on a valuable marketing resource and might be missing out on the chance to have hundreds of thousands of potential clients get to know them for the same cost it would to get one hundred people to know them. Financial advisors who are not utilizing online videos are very much marketing in a different era. An added benefit of using online videos is an improved website ranking on Google. That is why I had you video record your blog.

There are plenty of financial advisors out there who are unhappy with their website and the lack of calls generated by their site. It is a common misconception that building a fancy and expensive website will get potential clients to call. Videos are important because in addition to improving your search engine rankings and differentiating yourself from your competitors they offer some other key benefits.

Potential clients actually get to see you. Why do people watch TV? It is because they like to see the action. Articles are always a good tool, but personal video really enables the viewer to decide for himself or herself whether the financial advisor is right for them. An educational video is guaranteed to distinguish your business from your competitors.

Potential clients get to know you. A potential client who can hear how you speak, and see how you look, will start to feel comfortable with you. They will feel as if they already know you to a certain extent. Then, when they meet you in person, they will think of you as a familiar face rather than a complete stranger.

Familiarity fosters trust. A potential client who has viewed a video of you will be familiar with you and the way that you approach problems. All things being equal, the client is more likely to choose you as an advisor rather than some unknown advisor.

You are able to directly project your confidence to the viewer. Portraying confidence is a hard thing to do in text. It is much simpler and effective to do so in a video.

Prospective clients are able to learn about the ways in which you can help them. Prospective clients are not interested in how great you think you are. They have their own concerns and their own problems, and they want to know the ways in which you can help them. The most common form of thinking that financial advisors follow is that as a financial advisor, you want to show the client how knowledgeable and experienced you are. While it is important to be knowledgeable and experienced, you need to differentiate yourself from your competition or else your prospective clients will go elsewhere.

Ultimately, video is much more compelling than text. Most financial advisors are very similar. They have similar educational backgrounds and similar professional experiences. Every financial advisor has a website where they post articles and photos. How are you any different? You should begin to produce online videos now before your competition has time to catch up.

It is ok that your video is not professionally produced in a studio, though that is preferable. It is more important that you make one. We can help you with the scripting. Call, click, or email us.

Chapter 24
Direct Mail Millions

Isn't direct mail dead? Guess which Internet companies spend $Tens of Millions in direct mail through the good ol' US Postal Service? You would be correct if you said Google and Amazon. Why?

Direct Mail is a great way to identify your target market and speak directly to that person. You can be as specific as you like thanks to Big Data. It has been reported that more catalogs than ever appear in our mailboxes. And is it not more effective to speak to your potential target, who can further self identify, than to a whole mass of people, most of whom are not interested and not capable of qualifying to be your client?

By using the systems previously described you can expect a response rate of 0.25% to over 6% who become leads. Some may say that response rate is too low, or it is too expensive. I say, when done correctly, it is very profitable. Imagine sending out a campaign of three pieces to 1000 carefully selected potential clients.

XXXXX WEALTH **YYYYYY**, INC.
A Registered Investment Advisor
232-111-1234

Primum non nocere

Research consistently shows us that investors and retirees are frustrated – **physicians are too!** Expectations are not met, **asset protection** measures are not comprehensive, service is not prompt, detailed and proactive, and, in the end, relationships are not honored. However, many people just like you are benefiting from **a better way with Xxxxxx.**

Mr. First Advisor and **Mr. Second Advisor, CFP®** frequently encounter physicians and other professionals who are too busy to plan their future with confidence, they often aren't receiving **evidence-based information**, all of the information, or the **forward-thinking insight gained through Xxxxxx's proper Process of Discovery**.

> **Many important questions** are commonly not asked by CPAs, attorneys, money managers, brokers, and retirement planners – here are a few:
> - Have you identified *and* quantified **the true cost of all the fees and taxes in your investment accounts?** Have you determined how this will impact your long-term outlook?
> - Are you aware of, or affected by, **phantom income taxes?**
> - Is **your current investment risk an undiagnosed problem**, creating a ticking time-bomb in your financial future?
> - Do you have a tax-deferred annuity, qualified plan or significant **capital gains buildup** that you will not need for retirement income?
> - Do you take advantage of **tax harvesting strategies** such as offsetting losses with gains as well as properly using tax-deferred and tax-free strategies?

Call Today...

Contact First and Second direct at **232-111-1234** to arrange an introduction suitable to your schedule and **discover why so many people just like you recommend us.**

> "Those you care about in life are seeking important financial guidance from someone. Doesn't it make sense to work with someone you know, like and trust?"

Warm Regards,

Signatures

One Advisor   Other Advisor, CFP®

If each piece costs you $5, including packaging, copywriting, the list, postage, printing, that is $15,000. If you get only a 0.5% response rate, that is 5 people. If 5 people came to visit you, how many of them will become clients? 2? And what is your lifetime value of a client? Better yet, what is the 2-year value of that client?

Well, one $500,000 client at a 1% management fee is worth $5000 per year. Two such clients are worth $10,000 per year. After two years, you have delivered $20,000 of value, for only $15,000 cost. You see, it is worth it.

The higher response rate depends on your selects, and whether you are entering the conversation going on their mind. And it depends on whether it actually gets read.

So show up differently. Get your direct mail read. Only send to your most likely clients. Speak to them. Show them what is in it for them if they respond. If done wrongly, you may be disappointed. If done only once, you may be disappointed.

Use direct mail because it is so highly quantifiable, and measurable. You can tweak the envelope, the headline, the offer, the premium, the bonus, the calls to action, one at a time to get ever improving response rates.

Chapter 25
How To Write Your Book

Wait! What? Writing your own book may seem like an impossible task to most, however it is a very achievable goal and can have a profound impact on your business. Before writing a book, it is helpful to understand some of the most common problems that writers have, and the ways that you can get around them. It is also helpful to focus on the reasons why you are writing a book and what your expectations for it are after you have published it. With these thoughts in mind, you are on your way to successfully becoming a published author.

Being a published author can boost your credibility and respectability and also add to your client base by convincing potential clients that you are an expert in your field. A book is also valuable because it allows you to show potential clients that you are a person that they can trust and are able to offer wise counsel.

When, not if, members of the media cite you, they are able to make reference to the fact that you are a published author, which gives you additional clout. The most important benefit of writing a book is that you have something to give clients and potential clients that will solidify in their mind that you are an expert in your field.

When you begin writing your book, it is important to not think of it as writing a book at all. You should begin with a series of frequently asked questions about your practice area. If you think that the area is too broad, then focus on one area of your business that you spend a lot of your time on or an area that you really enjoy, and focus on that. Then spend about 45 to 90 minutes a day writing. This is a good amount of time because it allows your ideas to mature, but is not so long that you will lose focus.

As you go about the rest of your day, you should carry with you a notepad or recorder so that you are able to record any ideas that may come to you. When you begin your writing session for the day you should read out loud at least two pages of what you have previously written in order to get your mind into gear. Before you finish writing for the day, make sure that you know where you will begin the next day. This should help you avoid writers block, and will help you with your writing flow.

Make sure that you write in your own voice. People appreciate writing that sounds like it is from an actual person, so you should write like you normally speak. One great tip for writing is to write like you are talking to a person sitting across the table from you. Do not write as if you are speaking to an extremely large group of people. If you effectively write as if you are speaking to one person, then everyone who reads your book will understand that the book is written for them. In order to achieve this effect, some people find that it is best to dictate their writing. In any case, make sure that your writing reflects your personality.

When you begin writing, do not be overly concerned with how long your book is going to be. Some of the most successful self-published books are less than 100 pages. Many prospective clients lack the time to read a 250-500-page book; so don't panic if your book is not very long.

Reader friendly books are best; so make sure the writing is worth the reader's time. There is a common misconception that you have to be a truly great writer to produce your own book. This is not true. Your work does not need to measure up to Shakespeare or any other of the classics. Your writing simply needs to be clear and competent and showcase your business in a straightforward way.

There are some other things that you will want to keep in mind when you are publishing your book. You will have the option to publish in either hardback or soft cover. While you should plan on spending a few thousand dollars to publish a well-made book, it is not always worth the added expense of putting out a hardback. Trade paperbacks, which are slightly larger than typically paperbacks, offer the quality of a hardback book without the added expense.

Another aspect of your book that you need to pay attention to are the front and back covers. The back cover is almost as important as the front because it is generally where the reader turns their attention to after glancing at the front. It is typically a good idea for the author to put a picture of himself or herself on either the back cover or the last page of the book. The picture helps the reader feel like they know the author better.

Good financial advisors are always on the lookout for a marketing strategy that is completely original, one that will separate them from the competition. Writing a book is a great strategy since it is so different from other marketing tools. Other marketing strategies may get the word out, but they are limited. They are merely sound bites compared to the full story that you can present with a book. Writing a book will have a profound effect on your advisory business and is well worth the effort it takes.

If this is still too daunting, why not utilize a collaborative effort with some colleagues in different non-competing disciplines, or geographies? Or offer to present for, or co-write a book with a prolific writer. Or write his introduction, foreword, prologue, epilogue, or conclusion? One such book is my *"Science of Successful Investing Made Simple"*. Contact me to see how you may have your picture and name on that cover, or many other similar books, ready and completely done-for-you.

What To Do With Your Book

The obvious answer is to hand out the hard copy to your clients, potential clients, and centers of influence. Deliver two copies. They will deliver one for you.

Turn it into webinars. Turn it into videos for your YouTube channel. To help, you can use Animoto, VideoArticleRobot, VideoScribe and more. Pare it down into bite-sized bits for white papers, articles, blog posts, seminars, workshops, podcasts, and press releases. See the next chapter on public relations for more.

Display your book in your reception area and your conference room and your office. Refer to it often. Post it on your website prominently. You may offer to download the e-version from your website. You may try to sell it on your website, or on Amazon.

Chapter 26
Public Relations

Public Relations is more than just getting your company mentioned by the media, or a simple announcement about some award or promotion you received. It is a form of education and outreach that you can control. It is *free*, or can be if you do it yourself, though it takes a lot of work and attention to detail.

PR will provide you further third-party credibility and celebrity, so that when your potential new relationships are deciding whom to hire, they are more likely to choose you. They will choose you because they know you better, which helps them like and trust you more. And because the media outlets display you not as an advertiser but as a resource, they are more likely to trust you more as well. We choose what we know, like, and trust.

PR requires content. A lot of content. You will need relevant, topical and interesting content, which you will need to update frequently. If you don't know where to start, read a newspaper, magazine, or trade journal. You can also watch a show and comment to your spouse. Throughout this process you need to be *recording your comments*. Then have those comments transcribed. Then edit them. Then have someone else read them so you can be sure your communication is getting the response you want.

There is a formula you must follow. Again, it is a system. Follow it and succeed. Ignore or avoid or fail to use a system at your own peril.

The Content

In addition to comments, you can also source content from your book. Section it off. Create several white papers from it. From the white papers, create several articles of about 1500 words to submit to trade journals, newspapers, and the like. From these, further break them down to 300 – 500 word articles for submission to additional sources, which can include your local neighborhood newspaper, as well as other forms of media. From these, further cut them down to 75 – 150 word blog posts, or letters to the editors.

Do not forget to create videos, and podcasts, CDs, DVDs, and other media from the same content. And post, post, post all that content. You can post to Ezine, HARO, PRweb, Aweber, and so many more. Also, send out a press release with every post, about your post.

Slug: myths0714

Word count: 1,200

Images: 1

How to build a bomb-proof investment portfolio: The 10 myths that cause investors to fail

Excerpted as Part 1 from the forthcoming book *The Science of Successful Investing Made Simple*

by Mitch Levin, MD, CWPP, CAPP

Investing is a reality-based, evidence-based activity—or it should be. Unfortunately, for all too many investors, reality and evidence are circumvented by false ideas that prevent understanding and sound investment decision making. Ten myths in particular hamper the investor and need to be recognized for the false ideas that they are. Avoid these 10 fables and you will have a good start on the road to sound, scientific investment choices. Here are the myths:

1. Investment is a do-it-yourself project. Most investors not only lack the expertise, they also lack the discipline and the time necessary to properly develop, allocate, and manage their investment portfolios. The DALBAR research organization shows that investors continue to underperform by an astounding *3-7% annually* over any 20-year period of time.

2. You can get rich through investing. This rarely happens. If you're already rich and have a lot of money both to invest and to hire the best advice and management, you can get richer through investing, but for most people, whose capital for investment is limited, investment is a way of protecting assets and creating a fund for your goals, not a road to riches. Your gains will be a function of how much you have to invest, and a rate of return capable of turning modest means into great wealth is very unusual.

This is an example of a published article.

The Press Release

This should be one page only. Your headline has to be interesting. Your "bullet points" have to be interesting. You must have a body, and a way to contact you. Make sure you are available when you are contacted. You must make yourself available to the media. They need you and want you. The more you can spoon-feed them, the easier their job is and the more likely they will seek you out. The media is starving for good content. If you provide it, they will contact you and you will get interviewed.

As a financial advisor, keep in mind that potential clients do not know what your business is doing unless you tell them. Potential clients want to know about your business. Did you open a new location? Host a charity event? Have you made any outstanding new hires recently?

Unless you are telling your potential clients this information, there is no way for them to know. You will want to set up a news section on your website and on your social media pages where you can issue press releases. This will also make sure the information you are posting looks like news, and not self-promotion. Also, keep in mind that when you are writing a press release you will want to write it in the third person.

For Immediate Release

For Further Information Contact:
Mitch Levin
407/922-4689

(Headline—who cares?!) 17 Ways to Avoid an IRS Audit almost Instantly
12 Ways to Pick a Winning Stock almost Instantly

(Body copy) This year over 2.4 million tax payers will be audited by the IRS. 13,000 of them will be able to completely avoid it because they know the 3 steps to take. In this interview, you will learn
- first
- second
- third

(Quote) "It's true. Over 2.4 million people will be subject to an IRS audit. Most people don't have to go through this agony if they know the simple steps to take," says Mitch Levin, MD (the Financial Physician) a Certified Wealth Preservation Planner, and a "AA" rated Florida State Representative of the nationally recognized Asset Protection Society.

(Call to action) Attend a Free Workshop on Whatever It is that I will talk on at, 6PM Tuesday, July 5, 2009 to be held at the Public Library.
Or call the Free Hotline at 888-888-9999 for this weeks analysis.

(Also prepare a one page bio, and series of Q &A for the reporter)

This is an example of a press release template.

The Interview

Always tell the truth, the whole truth, and nothing but the truth. Do not be misleading or wishy-washy. Which means do not try to hide or change your personality, or your beliefs. They want controversy. Which means you are likely to attract some and repel others. That's ok. You will attract your ideal target audience.

Have a list of 3 key points you want to get across and be certain you turn every answer to them. This is what the political world calls spin or talking points or sound bites. Hone your message. Your three points, for example may be 1) have a plan 2) have an advisor, and 3) have disability insurance.

So, if you are asked if an IRA is a good investment, your answer could be "IRAs are good for some, but the best investment is to have plan, an advisor, and a disability insurance policy first".

The Media Kit

When a reporter contacts you, ask if you can send them a "media kit" if they do not ask you for one. If they are any good, they will ask you. A media kit includes:

A bio that is separate and different from your resume. See mine for example and feel free to swipe and deploy it for yourself with your own credentials. Shorter is better.

A prepared Q&A for the reporter, with the answers you want to give. This should be a list of about 25 questions. This saves the reporter time. And it shows you are not only prepared, but also that this is not your first rodeo.

CONTACT NUMBER: (407) 922-4689

Suggested Questions for Mitch Levin a *Leading Authority* in
How to be Outrageously Successful Financially, Almost Instantly

1. What makes you a Financial Physician?
2. What is Financial Coaching?
3. What are some of the biggest mistakes investors make?
4. What are the best investment strategies now?
5. How can anyone save 10's or even 100's of Thousands of $ in taxes?
6. (Follow up to # 7) Why haven't I heard of that?
7. (Follow up to # 8) Isn't that "too good to be true"?
8. How can I get a guaranteed return of 7%, without ever losing money?
9. How can your coaching make anyone an additional 6-8% per year?
10. I diversified, and still lost over 40% -- is diversification stupid?
11. Why do you say mutual funds are ripping us off in dozens of ways?
12. (Follow up to # 16) But you coach us to invest in mutual funds?
13. What are some of the expenses that are hidden in our 401(K)'s?
14. What's your best success story?
15. How can I (or my audience) get more information? (You can call me on my personal cell phone at 407/922-4689; or visit my website at www.LevinWealthSystems.com)

Suggested Introduction for Mitch Levin

Mitch Levin, MD is widely recognized as a leading authority in asset protection, tax reduction strategies, and successful investment coaching. He can tell you exactly how to achieve complete *Financial Freedom* quickly, and simply. As an MD, he is the Financial Physician, specializing in Healthy Investment Returns; in Financial Peace of Mind -- in helping you prosper and keep more of what you earn. Author, speaker, and Trusted Advisor, Dr. Mitch also often teaches attorneys and accountants. Be sure to have a pen and paper handy. He'll be giving you information you won't want to miss.

This is an example of the Q&A for reporters.

You should not expect instant miracles from PR. It takes time and hard work, even when outsourced. You are unlikely to get on Oprah. Even if you did, your appearance is unlikely to get you new clients. You may however get into the Wall Street Journal, USA Today, and Barrons. You may get on CNBC, FOX Business, and others.

I hope you do not feel overwhelmed. You are not required to do it all, and certainly not right now. You eat the elephant one bite at a time. Do something. Just get started. And do something else. And then keep doing it. If you would like help, contact our office. You will build, and possibly delegate this to your communications director. Over time it will work. PR will get you tangible new business.

Chapter 27
"The Shock and Awe" Package.

What do most financial advisors do when their marketing strategy pays off, and a prospective client requests more information from them? They will usually just send a brochure. What do you want to do? You want to shock them in order to create massive interest in your business.

When a potential client indicates that they want to hear more from you because you made them an irresistible offer in your marketing materials, they should receive a package that includes some of the following:

The book they requested from you.

A book that advises the reader on how to find an appropriate financial advisor for their needs.

An audio recording where you speak to clients.

A DVD of promotional material, or a television show on which you were interviewed.

A book of client testimonials.

Articles that you have written or have been written about you.

Your newsletters.

Press releases that your firm has issued.

It is always appreciated to include some kind of food goodie that is representative of your values. We have a client who is in the high-end chocolate manufacturing business, and includes one of his gift boxes with a note inserted inside.

You can package these materials in a box or envelope. While this approach will cost you some money, and your prospective client will most likely not read all of the material, it is important to keep in mind that people learn differently. Some learn information through reading, some by watching, and others by listening. Since you do not know what approach works best for each independent client, it is best to send it all.

And in keeping with the speed of trust, next day delivery is critical to showing up differently. It certainly is expensive and cumbersome to mail such a large package. But as a financial advisor, the transaction value of each client is high, so my advice is to not be cheap on this issue.

Chapter 28
Financial Advisors
and Other Social Media

These days, financial advisors ignore social media at their peril. Just because you might not notice a trend, does not mean that it's not there and happening. Even though you may not be focused on it at all times, does not mean that the online world is not always on.

Recently, social media has had an even greater effect as groups well outside the typical college crowd have widely adopted it. Many predicted that social media would only be adopted by a youthful demographic. While this may have been the case initially, many more people have been signing up for sites such as Twitter, LinkedIn and Facebook. The age gap is narrowing as more people who are no longer college age join and encourage others that they know to join as well. Thousands of people in the United States of all ages join social media every day. The people joining come from all walks of life, and they connect with people throughout their communities.

Using the excuse that your consumer base is not on Facebook, or any other form of social media is a dangerous attitude to take in today's hypercompetitive online marketing world. Arguing that Twitter is beneath you is an old school attitude. The train is leaving the station. Do you want to be on it?

For some, social media remains an unfamiliar concept. Loosely defined, social media is a way for individuals and businesses to express themselves and communicate with each others in an online community. While there are hundreds of sites out there that would fall under the umbrella of social media, it benefits your business to find the most effective ones. I would suggest that you start with LinkedIn, Twitter, Facebook and YouTube. Blogs can also be considered to be part of social media.

Social networking is a way that many people utilize social media services. Think of social media as the way people broadcast messages and social networking as the communicating and connecting that happens on social media. Utilize social media to increase your social networking capabilities.

Social media, and the Internet in general, have fundamentally changed the way that people interact with one another. It has become standard practice to share what you read, watch and listen to. People also share general experiences. These include what countries they have visited, the meals they have cooked and what companies they do business with.

Let's examine some marketing building blocks:

Introductions: When you build your client base, you are not just adding to the list of people who do business with you. You are also adding a list of people that can recruit potential clients. Referred client introductions are often times great clients. Social media is a great way for happy clients to sing your praises. You should make that easy for them.

Client Reference List- This is the ultimate social medium. Direct social contact between potential clients and existing clients. If you are not directly introduced by an existing client, then you should try to get a list to share with potential clients. Be sure that you obtain permission from the person(s) giving you the reference. And be sure not to advertise this list. Advise your potential clients not to ask, and your existing clients not to share personal information such as how much they have, or what you have done for them. They should simply say something like, "these are the people I know, like, and trust." Be judicious in your use of this list so as not to bother your existing clients. And use extreme caution not to share it on other forms of media you are using, including online and offline publications.

Being Found- People like to shop around when looking for a financial advisor, and the first resource that they consult when making a decision is the Internet. Google is in the business of returning the most relevant results. Sometimes the most relevant result is a posting from social media.

Information- Potential clients like to be well informed before they choose a financial advisor. You need ways to deliver useful information to a potential client before they have the time to go to another place to gain information.

Interactions: The one-on-one interactions that you have with potential clients are integral to gaining new customers.

Reputation: Having control of your reputation is of the utmost importance. No one is going to hire a financial advisor who they think is untrustworthy. Having many clients can help offset that one negative comment that one disgruntled client may have lobbed at you. If you have license dings, or lawsuits, avoid social media. In fact, consider changing careers.

Each of these categories is enhanced by a presence on social media. Maintaining your presence on social media and using effective social media strategies can be an important move to increasing the profit level of your business.

The fact that all generations have embraced social media has made it a great place for introductions. A Facebook page or Twitter handle can easily be shared, but only if you are using those networks. Be sure that all your social media profiles have the option to give effective online introductions.

Being discovered on the Internet requires a combination of search engine optimization and social media enhancement. All well-known search engines use algorithms that take social media into account. The practical effect is that if you want to show up high on a search, you will need a social media presence. Many businesses' social media profiles play an active part in their showing up on the front page of Google.

Distributing valuable, topical and timely free information is a great way to build your reputation as an expert in your field. Using social media allows you to serve your clients better in two ways. First, you are widely broadcasting your information, which makes it easy for people in need of that information to find it. And second, broadcasting that information allows people who are merely curious to access your information and access it later if they ever have a need for it.

Since there are so many different ways people communicate these days, it is important that you be able to facilitate communication in many different arenas. Social media allows you to rapidly communicate with a large number of people without ever having to send an email. Social media has the added benefit of being public, which means that your information can be found by others who may have the same questions. As your social media web grows, you will begin to notice that other people have good things to say about you online. These positive referrals will continue to grow as time goes on and you expand your network.

One of the keys to having a successful financial advisory business is to maintain a great reputation. As more forms of communication move online, it is likely that your business will be brought up at some point. If you do not make an effort to establish yourself on social media, then people will be able to disparage you, and you won't even have the opportunity to respond.

Most social media sites do not charge anything to sign up and are not difficult to learn how to use. They can greatly enhance and expand your marketing efforts. If you do not make the effort to expand your online presence, including social media, you will be at a disadvantage to competitors who have.

Weathering Criticism

Some great ways to surpass your competition are to remain client-centric at all times, create key brand associations and to always utilize your core values. While these are all key components to attaining success, if you stop here, you will never reach the upper echelons of financial advisors.

Consider this hypothetical: You run a client-centered practice that has a perfect record of fiduciary service toward your clients. Despite this impressive track record of success and diligence, an anonymous commenter has begun a campaign against you on the website Yelp. He is posting disparaging remarks claiming that you have consistently failed to provide attentive customer service.

In your everyday practice, if a client were to raise an issue about the level of customer service to you or one of your employees, you would be in a position to take immediate action and address the client's concerns head on. A direct complaint is something that you can tackle. But how do you deal with anonymous web criticism, or other forms of faceless criticism lobbed your way.

Anonymous criticism is unlike angry emails or phone calls. While the criticisms left on sites like Yelp or Angie's List may have no basis in reality, even unfounded accusations have the possibility to remain on the Internet in perpetuity.

The Susceptible Reputation

Left untreated, the existence of free-floating criticism has the power to suffocate the air out of your business. It can devour good will you have accumulated and cause irreparable damage to your brand.

While long-term clients may not be dissuaded from doing business with you just because of a few negative Internet comments, prospective clients very well may. The fact of the matter is that there are very few ways in which a prospective client is able to assess your character and judge whether you run a reputable business. Unless negative comments are countered by overwhelmingly positive feedback or pushback from loyal and satisfied clients who know the strength of your integrity, there is a very real chance that even comments that lack a hint of truth may damage your business in ways that make it difficult for you to counter.

Tackling the Criticism Preemptively

It is not possible for you to effectively counter free-floating criticism on Internet sites by refuting the criticism in the comment pages beneath the post. This could not only get you into trouble with the regulatory authorities, but also is unlikely to be persuasive to any potential client.

As a financial advisor, it is important that you take proactive damage control measures because reactive measures are less effective and subject to more constrictions. Keeping this in mind, countering free-floating criticism is much easier done when the public is well informed about your firm's core values. So, to fortify your business against negativity you need to actively involve yourself in your community's charity life. (See Chapter 29).

Don't Ignore the Gossip

Websites like Yelp use algorithms that give more attention to a negative review than to a positive one. This means that there is a chance that people searching for your company may come across a negative comment before they come across a positive one.

Studies have shown that negative reviews can affect the bottom line, costing some businesses as much as 20 percent of their revenues.

Search engines like Google also use complicated algorithms that are capable of detecting negative information throughout the Internet. If you receive a bad review, Google, among other search engines, will move your website further down its list of relevant content. If enough negative content is compiled, the search engine is likely to remove you from its search results altogether. In today's Internet age, if you are removed from Google's search results you might as well be living in a cave, since the same amount of people will be able to find you.

While you may not be overly concerned with one negative review, what will you do if you get more? Numerous bad reviews very well could begin to dig into your bottom line. Are you prepared to drop down in the Google search results, or even off Google altogether?

Where would your business be without the support of your community and no Google referrals? Just think of where your business could be with a client centric approach, published core values, numerous positive online reviews, and a reputation for deep community involvement.

Chapter 29
Community Involvement

The Intersection Between Giving and Your Practice

IMPORTANT WARNING: Do not be "that guy". You know who I mean. The guy with sales-breath. It will ruin your position of trust. Remember, you are doing this for the charity. You may just happen to develop good relationships that may eventually translate into business as a byproduct. However, this should NOT be the primary purpose.

Many people believe that all acts of charity need to be entirely selfless endeavors. This is not necessarily true. Sometimes giving makes you feel good. So, actually you are taking something. Just because the giver of charity benefits in some way does not diminish the importance of the act of giving.

(Notice I did not say, "giving back". Nobody gave you your success. You earned it. So there is nothing to give back. Don't let someone try to make you feel guilty. You sacrificed; you spent your capital, your labor, your risk to succeed. To the extent you have extra resources you wish to share, then by all means give it.)

But do not forget, after all, you are *giving to the charity*, primarily.

You will, as a happy coincidence, result, effect, and through the principle of reciprocity, get something in return. You will probably even gain more business opportunities. However, if you are seeking to receive something as the primary purpose of your involvement in charities, please skip this chapter.

Charities need people like you. Many charities rely on funds raised from the business community to meet their yearly expenses. But aside from purely financial support, you are in possession of numerous skills that can be advantageous to a charity organization.

It is also important to remember that the charities themselves recognize that there are many considerations that a benefactor considers when choosing to donate their time or money. This is not a bad thing. Both the charity and the benefactor benefit from the arrangement.

In the end, you want to give to charities with the best and noblest intentions. You should not feel guilt or doubt when that act of giving, later on, benefits your business. However, if that is your primary purpose, don't. You definitely don't want to be "that guy". It will backfire badly.

Evidence That Your Strategy Is Paying Off

You cannot accurately gauge reputation only by assets under management. You also can't allow anonymous Internet reviewers, who, for all you know, may be your competition, determine the success or failure of your business. While your current clients may think the world of you, the reality is that many of them will keep their opinions of you to themselves.

I joined the Orlando area Association for Corporate Growth (ACG), because I am passionate about the quality of our community and concerned with the comparatively low level of business development in Central Florida. Many of our clients are business owners. I have written a book for them, "Payday! Your Business Sold. You Have Sudden Wealth™. Now What?" ACG is the only non-governmental group dedicated to helping businesses grow, by connecting them and their professional advisors with sources of capital to propel them to the next level. I am on the membership committee as of this writing.

My purpose in involving myself with ACG is not to obtain business. And that is precisely why business comes to our firm. We have been introduced to over $150 Million in opportunity over the last 12 months. Is it because of ACG? Perhaps it is because we are "out there" on behalf of our community. You can do something like this too.

Measuring the Amount of Your Community Involvement

As a financial advisor, you more than likely classify your clients by how much money they have invested with you. It makes organizational sense for you to separate your clients into different group because each group may require a different level of service.

Think about community service in the same way. The more that you give to a particular charity, the more the charity receives from you. The opposite is also true. The more you have invested in a charity, the greater professional and personal benefit you stand to gain.

There are different levels of commitment when it comes to charitable contributions. While you typically would rank your clients monetarily, when it comes to community involvement, time and expertise hold greater cache than monetary contributions alone. You want to measure your commitment by activity.

Three Levels of Community Involvement

Money

Money, time, and expertise

Money, time, expertise, and sponsorship

First Level Involvement

First-level commitment is when you give a financial contribution to a charitable organization. There is nothing wrong with this approach. It is great to help a charitable organization financially, and it will also probably give you some good publicity. However, the drawback to this approach is that it is a relatively hands-off approach.

Hopefully a time will come in your career where you have more resources to devote to charities than there is time in the day.

However, if you are just getting started with your community involvement, or you are looking to start expanding your involvement incrementally, you should be on the lookout for a single charity and make it your goal to grow together.

Simply donating money is fine, but ultimately it is not the most beneficial arrangement for either the charity or for you. You have much more to offer a charity than just money alone.

Second Level Involvement

It is entirely possible for you to further involve yourself with a charitable organization and make an even greater impact. For example, you find a charity whose principles and goals you really admire. You decide to not only contribute financially to the charity, but to also contribute your time and expertise to helping the charity grow. You use your knowledge and contacts as a financial advisor to help the charity fundraise, or maybe even offer to help them with some basic bookkeeping.

This would be an example of second level involvement. Not only are you contributing funds to the organization, but you are also directly involving yourself in the operations of the charity. You are providing a unique skill set that the charity would have a hard time finding elsewhere. The great thing about being directly involved with a charity is that you are likely to meet other people who have the same mind set as you are working to get them involved with the charity. This is a great networking opportunity. Overall, second level involvement allows you to increase your network, elevate your brand and grow the reach of your company. While second level involvement is great, it is still not the best that you can do.

Third Level Involvement

If at all possible, you want to be at the third level of involvement. This involves combining all the actions that you have taken in the first and second level of involvement, and using them to facilitate a major fundraising event or growth initiative through sponsorship.

As you can see, the third level of involvement benefits all parties the most. Within your community you will be associated with progress, good acts, and charity. While charitable acts alone cannot shield you from criminal or unethical behavior, your public involvement in helping the community will give you the benefit of the doubt. What you are doing is making your business less susceptible to free-floating criticism, while at the same time improving your community and helping the people in it.

If you are a new business, then it is unlikely that you would start at the third level of involvement, however there is always the possibility. What is great about the third level is that your monetary contributions are the least important thing. Each level requires that you give money, however for the second and third level your time, expertise and fundraising ability will be much more valuable to the charity than any amount of money you could give. This is great news for a new firm.

The practical meaning of all this is that you have the greatest effect when you are giving of yourself and working your way into a position of leadership rather than writing a check and buying your way in.

Finding Great Charities and Projects

For our purposes here, we have conflated charity and philanthropy; non-profit and tax-exempt. They are not the same. But that is another book. Charities come in 5 general types, in order of how much money they attract: 1) religious 2) educational 3) health care 4) social services 5) arts. The arts can be broken down further to a) museums b) philharmonics c) theater d) ballet e) opera.

Our passion is opera. Do you have one?

A great way to find potential charities to get involved with is to solicit your client's advice. This allows you to not only compile a list of great charities but also will enhance your relationships with your clients and foster a deeper bond.

What if none of the client's suggestions for charities are appropriate for your needs? What is your next move?

Fortunately, you will more than likely be solicited for charitable contributions on a regular basis. However, the process of vetting all of these offers can be time consuming, and pull your attention away from your business. You also want to be on guard for phone solicitations, even from charities that you recognize. Charities that utilize phone solicitation as a means of fundraising have typically outsourced their phone solicitation operation to a third party. This third party will generally charge a percentage of all the dollars that it brings in to the charity. There is clearly a possible potential conflict of interest here.

In order to save you time and give you peace of mind, there are a number of organizations that perform the necessary due diligence on each charity.

Your goal here is to form a partnership with the charity that you select. It is absolutely imperative that you partner with a charity that holds the same high standards of ethical behavior that you do. Any whiff of impropriety from the charity that you partner with could carry on to you. Always remember that the company you keep has the possibility of enhancing or degrading your reputation. Remember to review the by-laws, visit with board members and senior staff, read the rules, and by all means avoid even the perception of conflicts of interest.

The point is that no matter where the idea to partner with a particular charity originates, be it a client, a COI, a solicitor, or the phonebook, you need to do a certain amount of due diligence on that charity. You should visit the charity and speak with their employees and volunteers. Also seek out the target demographic of the charity. These are the people who that particular charity has targeted to help. Interview them. Find out if they are being helped, and their overall opinion of the charity. If you are getting positive feedback from all of these sources, then you should target the community that the charity is located in. Does the charity enjoy a solid reputation amongst its' neighbors?

How to Vet a Charity

- Do an Internet search

- Visit the charity in person

- Review the mission statement

- Ask for and review the financial statements

- Make a donation to ensure that the charity is efficient

- Understand the base and sources of financial support

- Interview the charity's employees and volunteers

- Interview people in the charity's target demographic

- Interview people in the community in which the charity is located.

Signs of a Problem

There is always the possibility with charities that they lose some of their steam. They start out strong and attract a lot of attention. They are able to raise a considerable amount of money, but then they lose their effectiveness.

While the charity may have in mind financial stability, it is this very thought that may be the end of that charity's viability.

Charities, like businesses in the for-profit sector, often times become bloated and wasteful. They also become vulnerable to corruption and mismanagement.

Even the founders of charitable entities can become corrupted by access to money. While their charities may have been founded with the purest intentions, overwhelming success may have them feeling overconfident, and they may lose sight of why they started their charity in the first place. These are the types of charities that you want to avoid. Do not partner with charities that have become complacent. Just because they have done good acts in the past does not mean that they will continue those acts in the future. There is a very real possibility that a charity like this will fail, and you do not want to be there when it does.

Selecting A Location

For a number of reasons, local charities are preferable to non-local charities. Hopefully you will be spending a lot of time at the charity, and for convenience sake, you should make sure that the charity is easy to access. Also, non-local charities will more than likely not be targeting your local community for its' initiatives. In order to grow your own profile among the community it is important for the charity you partner with to have an active presence in that community.

Management

People with extensive private sector experience often run some of the best charities. This is because they have experience in organizations that prioritize efficiency, short turnaround times, and specific goals. Be sure that any charity you partner with have a written mission statement that has a clearly defined message.

Many charities have an admirable goal, but are so mismanaged that they have no practical way of meeting that goal.

Mixing Causes

Whatever charity you choose to partner with, be sure that the focus of the charity, as well as the principals of the charity, are aligned with your professional and personal convictions. As a business owner, you want to appeal to the largest audience that you can. While having strong personal, political or religious beliefs is admirable, you do not want to appear militant or unreasonable. You face possible scandal if the charity you involve yourself with openly advocates for something controversial or political.

Make sure that you are pragmatic when choosing a charity. You want to choose a charity that helps your community, not one that will alienate half of your client base. Your first goal should be to help others, with the byproduct being that you are raising your own visibility within the community. If you espouse a controversial viewpoint, do not be surprised if clients choose to leave or prospective clients go elsewhere because they do not find your views compatible with their own. You want to select a charity to partner with that is inclusive and that everyone can admire.

Things to Look for in a Charity

1. Recommended by a Client

2. Tax-exempt

3. Located locally

4. Well defined goals and mission statement

5. A sterling reputation

6. Staffed by people who really care about their work

7. Non-political

8. Will accept your help and ask for it when they need it

Beginning You Community Involvement

You want to begin your community involvement as soon as it is practical. Do not rush into a situation that you are unsure of, or one that makes you uncomfortable. Because of your profession and unique skill set, most charities will welcome your involvement with open arms.

Make sure that you are confident that you have chosen the right charity. Also approach this with the perspective that you are choosing a charity to partner with, so your involvement will be long term. If you are unable to find a charity that you are one hundred percent confident with, do not just make a random decision. There are other avenues that you can pursue

Museums

In most cities throughout the United States, local government supports the arts in some way. While recently there have been a proliferation of for-profit museums, the majority of traditional museums are non-profit organizations that rely on the patronage of local community members for fundraising and growth. While supporting a museum is not a direct substitute for becoming heavily involved with a local charity, it is nonetheless a worthy endeavor. Many people are of the opinion that museums enrich civil society.

The ideal form of giving as it relates to you and your business would be to give to an organization that helps individuals, but donating to an organization like a museum will also benefit yourself and your business. If you are unable to find a charity to partner with, consider joining the board of a local museum. In addition to helping the museum, this will provide you a networking opportunity, and you may very well be able to find a charity with which you can become involved through your involvement on the museums board.

You should not find it difficult to become involved with your local museum. Most museums will have a department dedicated to local outreach efforts. Simply find a museum that you like, go to the website, and make a call to them.

Libraries

Although some believe libraries are becoming obsolete, nothing could be further from the truth. Many cities continue to build more libraries as they make efforts to refurbish and revamp currently existing libraries. Library patronage has also continued to rise in many cities.

In many ways, libraries act as meeting points for a local community. In addition to their traditional lending services, many libraries have added e-book loans as well as free Internet access, DVD and music loans. Libraries also typically have a vast archive of art, film collections and historical artifacts. They are host to many events that cater to a diverse clientele. All of these activities require funding, organization, and promotion in order to succeed.

Libraries generally are funded by endowments, which are enhanced by local contributions. There are numerous opportunities for you to become involved. Many of the same types of people who are involved with fundraising for local museums are involved with fundraising efforts at local libraries. However, there is one important difference. Many libraries specifically cater to children. This will add to the number of ways that you can become involved and have a local impact.

Community Involvement And Your Employees.

Numerous studies have shown that companies that are active in their local community are more successful in attracting and retaining top talent. Studies have also shown that companies that encourage community involvement have higher satisfaction levels than companies that do not. Many of the same benefits of volunteering that are applicable to charities and benefactors also carry over to employees. Some of these include

Volunteerism strengthens an employee's identification with your firm.

Volunteering improves employee morale.

Volunteering helps employees meet emotional and professional needs that work is unable to satisfy.

Volunteering broadens employee's horizons, providing a unique experience.

Volunteering rallies employees together, making them a more cohesive unit.

It is not realistic to think that every one of your employees will love their job. Some personality types will always view work as an obligation that has to be fulfilled, no matter how taxing.

A great way to keep employees engaged in their work is to involve them in projects that are greater than themselves. Community involvement is a great way to accomplish this mission. Not only does it improve upon the overall work experience but it also makes your company matter to the employee beyond a paycheck. As you move to become more involved in your local community, you want to be sure that you are bringing your employees along with you.

One of the best ways to accomplish this is to encourage your employees to volunteer with the charity that you have chosen to partner with. Make sure that you first confirm that your employees are interested. You should visit the charity with your employees during regular business hours. Make sure that you clearly explain the charity's mission, and then ask whether your employees would be interested in giving their time to the charity. Hopefully volunteering will prove to be a satisfying activity for your employees and they will be able to appreciate their work and the world in a new light. They will also return to work refreshed and will be appreciative of the opportunity that you helped facilitate. When your employees become involved in the volunteer effort, it strengthens the bond between the charity, your firm, and the employee.

Involvement at The Office

Sometimes it is just not possible for you to commit the amount of time necessary for level three involvement. Luckily, there are plenty of events that you can hold at your own office that will not only increase morale but also will allow you to set the groundwork for greater involvement at a later date.

Blood Drives

March of dimes collections

Canned food drives

Raising money for the Fireman's foundation

Organizing a team for a charity race

Ideally you would begin your contribution to a charity in a large-scale format in which you could add events like the ones mentioned above. The reason being is that almost any business could hold a canned food drive. The unique skill set that you bring to the table as a financial advisor combined with the marketing limitations that effect financial advisors make the ideal approach to charity involvement a large scale one.

Doing It Yourself

Choosing to partner with a charity means that you will be working within the parameters of an existing framework. Your prospective partners may or may not be open to listening to your ideas. This can be a major turn-off for some people, so it is important to recognize that there are alternatives.

There is always the possibility of founding your own charity. This is no easy feat. If you are just beginning to develop your own business, running a charity will pull you away from that endeavor for significant periods of time. You may find yourself overburdened, and unable to make either your practice or charity a success. If you do not have the luxury of spending at least half of your time on your charity, then you are probably not in a position to start one.

There are other ways to involve yourself in the community where you are able to expand your brand and remain in control.

Organizing Your Own Event

There are countless fundraising, brand-enhancing events that you can organize. Some examples may include a tennis tournament or a Charity Walk/Ride/Race. Golf tournaments are overdone, difficult, time and labor and capital consuming, and ultimately result in lower than expected charitable contributions. Look for alternatives. They are numerous. Contact me if you get stuck.

Sponsorships

My wife and I sponsor the Metropolitan Opera National Council Auditions and the Orlando Philharmonic Orchestra's concert opera performances several times a season. We invite about 60-80 people to our house for dinner and wine and opera and other vocal and classical entertainment. It is costly, about $7000 per event all in. It is what we enjoy, and what we feel we can best do to help our community.

You do not have to go that far. Your sponsorship could be a $300 golf hole at a local charity event (though that is often under-appreciated by the attendees). For more on this, send me an email.

Press

It is easier than you may have imagined for you to get publicity for your event. You need to start early. Many news stations devote a significant amount of their airtime covering local human-interest stories. News stations have a lot of airtime that they need to fill and your charity event offers them a perfect opportunity to cover an event that is helping the local community.

If you find yourself as the point person for press recruiting, it is important to remember that perseverance is key. Local news anchors and columnists will have public email addresses. You should contact them early and often, always emphasizing the charity aspect of your event. Keep at it and you will see results.

Mission Statement of the Event

Be sure to write a mission statement for your event that properly captures the ideals and aims of your event. Keep this statement very basic. The idea here is to spell out your intentions in a way that everybody can understand, so that you are able to effectively distribute your message.

We recognize that you are a busy professional. Giving takes time and effort. It may be easy for you to say to yourself, I simply do not have time for this. Often times the hardest thing is to take the first step. Once you take the first step to involving yourself in a charity, it often becomes much easier to find the time. If you become involved, you will be benefiting the charity, your community, your brand, your employees, your business and yourself.

Chapter 30
How To Track Your Marketing Efforts and Results

It is very important to track the results of your marketing campaign. Knowing what attracted your clients allows you to make an informed decision when deciding where to spend your marketing dollars. There will be plenty of salesmen trying to sell you ad space in different forms of media, and it is important that you are well informed when making a decision. When making a decision about marketing expenditures, financial advisors should look at the return on investment.

Only direct response marketing allows you to quantify, measure and analyze your efforts. You should expect your outbound outreach efforts to deliver a minimum of 3 to 1 return on revenue to expense. Some marketers will tell you a lower ratio is ok. That is not acceptable. That is a recipe for business failure. You must experience positive cash flow as a result of your marketing efforts within the same fiscal year.

Marketing for a financial advisor should be twofold. You should be marketing to attract clients now, but you should also be marketing to people you will sign as clients later down the road by finding the names and addresses of people who find you interesting. These people may not be in the market for a financial advisor today, but building a list of people who are interested in you and who might think of you when they are in the market is vital. This list is one of your most important assets. It is the beginning of your herd.

If you are running an advertisement where you break even in terms of the clients you are signing immediately, but you are able to gain names for your prospective client database, then overall, your marketing piece is net-positive. The only question then is whether there is another type of advertisement that you could be running that gets an even better return on investment.

Keep in mind that you do not want to rely on any *one* form of advertisement in your marketing practice. It would not be prudent to rely solely on the Yellow Pages or solely on the Internet. We do not know if these avenues to advertise will exist in their current form in the future, or whether they will exist at all. Even in most of our lifetimes, the way people search for a financial advisor has changed drastically. What you want to try and establish is a portfolio of marketing messages and media that will allow you to achieve an overall great result.

Here are the ways you can keep track of your marketing results.

Specialized tracking of phone numbers. There are numerous firms from which you can purchase a local or toll free number. You are then able to keep track of the number of people who call your line. The drawback to this approach is that the number you purchased may be used over and over again by the same people, thus giving you an unreliable result.

Tracking URLs. This allows you to create landing pages that are assigned to a particular URL. You will then be able to know when a consumer fills out a web form, exactly what advertisement piece they saw or heard before going on the Internet.

Tracking web forms. Set up web forms that ask for contact information or make offers for your book or media package throughout your websites. Every web form can be tracked so that you know which page each unique visitor came through. It is possible for you to completely automate this process.

Ask the prospective client. Of all the methods, this is the least precise. Clients may not fully remember where they saw your advertisement, even though they give you an answer.

The main idea is that when we are deciding where to spend our time and dollars, we want to know what has been working and what will work. We also want to remember to diversify our marketing efforts.

Chapter 31
Call Recording and Management

In today's hypercompetitive world, financial advisors have to manage their marketing budget more closely than ever. It is essential for the modern financial advisor to hone in on their message and launch a targeted marketing campaign.

Many financial advisors do not take this approach. Unfortunately, their marketing campaigns are more scattershot. They look to see what the financial advisor down the street is doing, and simply copy their competitor. If they see another financial advisors taking out a radio advertisement, then they will take out a radio advertisement because they assume that it is working. What they are not doing is the necessary research to determine whether this approach will work for them. They may even take out multiple forms of advertisement, but not take the time to track which advertisements are winners, and which ones are losers.

An especially dangerous proposition is when a small or midsize financial advisor attempts to copy the marketing strategy of a much larger competitor. They are trying a branding strategy when they should be trying to generate leads and converting leads to sales. Unless you are Apple or GE, you cannot rely on a brand name to grow your business. National branding campaigns are enormously expensive, well beyond the means of your typical mid-size financial advisor.

A better strategy, and a much more cost effective one, is for financial advisors to use call management and recording services to track the success of each marketing campaign.

Call measurement is an essential component in any advertising or marketing campaign. Without it, business owners are unable to track where the clients they sign are coming from. This means that they will have to continue to spend the same amount of money each month on advertisements in order to keep the flow of new clients the same. This is highly inefficient. You should only be spending money on advertisements that are actually bringing your business clients. Call measurement is a great tool because you are able to hold the advertising agencies accountable for the response rates that they recommend and sell you on.

Call measurement systems enable financial advisors to pinpoint where responses are coming from, which advertisements prospective clients are attracted to, and what made the prospective client contact them. Call measurement allows the financial advisor to determine which ad campaigns are working, and which campaigns are duds. This system enables you to spend more efficiently and gives you a better return on investment, which ultimately means more profit for your business.

Call measurement works by starting with a new, unique telephone number that is different from your office number, which you can place in your advertisements. Then, when the potential client sees your marketing material and calls the unique number, results from the individual marketing campaigns can be compared against the results from other marketing campaigns.

When a potential client calls from one of the tracked numbers, additional information is also captured. This information typically includes that caller's name, number, address and some other basic demographic information. The most important thing is the advertisement that generated the call is tracked.

Call Recording

Any financial advisor looking for a more efficient marketing strategy can benefit from call recording. Call recording allows business owners to increase their employee's skills and increase the conversion rate of callers to clients.

It is common for many financial advisors, when they feel that their marketing campaigns are not producing the results that they desire, to cut their marketing budget and reallocate the money to a different area of their business. In some of these cases, the marketing campaigns are not working because the financial advisor is not keeping track of their marketing efforts, but in many cases it is because incoming calls are being handled poorly.

Each marketing campaign may generate hundreds of responses, but typically only a small percentage of those responses ever reach the company. Sometimes the calls are not handled correctly.

Was the call answered in a timely manner? Did the person who answered the call attempt to turn the potential client into an actual client? Was the potential client offered the shock and awe package, or were they just given the same basic information that every other financial advisor gives out. Was there any attempt to build trust?

Financial advisors who implement call recording tend to see performance ratios increase. This is because the employees know that management is listening. Call recording is an accountability tool as well as a training tool. A financial advisor may use call recording for training purposes in addition to evaluating how well the call was handled.

The easy button for prospective clients is to avoid talking to a sales person. No one likes to be sold. Everyone likes to buy. Recall the last time you went into a men's clothing store? "Just looking", you said. Right. Your prospective clients feel the same way. Have available a 24/7 recordable message system for them to leave the address for you to deliver the book, DVD, white paper, or article they requested, that does not include a live attendant.

Mitchell Levin

Chapter 32
Direct Response Radio Advertising.

Radio advertising is an underappreciated asset in the financial advising world. It is difficult to find something that currently works on the radio and consistently brings in clients year after year. However, radio is very good at targeting specific groups and communicating principle information. Radio also removes consumer objections from the equation and raises awareness of you among potential clients, all in a positive manner.

The most effective form of advertising, again, is direct-response, not the expensive brand-building. The ability to determine which ads, running on which station, are pulling the most responses from potential clients is essential to tracking your return on investment. Direct response radio advertisements draw responses from potential clients immediately.

Many financial advisors use direct response radio ads to facilitate book or information requests, which then allow the financial advisor to place the respondent in their marketing sequence.

While this process may sound simple, it takes a lot of time and effort to create a great radio advertisement.

Make sure that you pick a radio station that targets your ideal client. Also, be sure that the ad covers your preferred geographic area and choose what you feel is the appropriate number of times listeners are offered the chance to respond to your ad. One pitfall to keep in mind is that you do not want to adopt the strategy of simply picking the radio station that you listen to most frequently. Your potential clients may not have the same tastes, and you are marketing to them, not yourself.

Radio divides the day into 4 or 5-hour segments: Morning Drive, Midday, Afternoon, Evening and Overnight. You need to determine what time of day the station has the most listeners of the type you want to target. You will also want to research if there is any special programming on the station such as call in shows that might be relevant to your business. Also, be sure to ask the sales team if there are any other products available such as bonus ads or web-links. Finally, research what community events the radio station is involved in that might tie into your financial advisory or the charitable contributions that you give.

When you build your ad schedule, make sure that you own at least one or two day parts or features weekly. If you are running ads on a music channel, then a wise strategy would be to run 2 ads per day for five weekdays during one 4 hour period or three ads per day for at least 3 weekdays during a single period. If you are advertising on a talk/sports/news station you will want to run ads on a certain show hourly in order for the listeners to get to know you and associate you with a particular show. You will want to advertise at least two weeks per month. You can experiment with which weeks you advertise, and determine what works best for you.

It is important to put a lot of thought into how you craft your message. Always keep your objective in mind: sharing how to get your book, or other free material, and why that material is important. Incorporate one-way to respond websites or phone numbers so that you are able to keep track of how your ad is doing. Only air one ad at a time unless you have a high frequency schedule for each ad. Airing more than one ad per schedule weakens your frequency and makes your ad less effective.

Consider participating in promotional giveaways the station might offer. You can package up marketing material like your book along with other desirable items such as dinner at a great local restaurant. It's not necessarily important who receives the giveaway. What is important is the publicity that goes along with the giveaway. Many radio stations do these promotional giveaways for free, and I don't know many people who object to getting publicity for free.

If you think that the day your ad first hits the air is the end of your work, then you would be mistaken. This is only the beginning of capitalizing on the momentum your campaign will generate. The next step will be for you to track your responses. You will want to use your client database system to record each contact received from the ad campaign along with the time and date it was received. Make sure that you inquire how the prospective client heard about your business. Record the city and state where the caller is from, and ask them what their favorite radio stations are. You will find this information useful when deciding where to expand your ads to next. The final step will be to record how many calls were received each day, week, and month. Use this information to cross-reference the times at which you are advertising.

With so many avenues of communication available to the average person, a potential client is able to look up your phone number, website and business in any number of ways, so it is very important to ask callers how they heard about you. Radio advertisements will bolster other forms of advertisement that you are doing, so you will want to refer back to your baseline to see what effect your radio advertising has on all means of contact you have for your business.

You always want to be refining your radio advertising campaign. Don't feel that you have to make changes immediately; back up any hypothesis you have with hard data, and don't change more than one thing at a time. If you get no responses after two weeks of running your ads, change and have your ads run on only one or two days. You may also want to look at changing the wording of your ad as well as the time of day your ad runs, or even the station. Remember to only change one thing at a time. This will help you determine what is the most effective message to your clients, and the areas in which to target potential clients most effectively.

Once you have a decent number of potential clients coming in, it is easy to increase your market share. You can add more ads to a different part of the day, place ads on a different station or go after a different niche.

Make sure you start tracking potential clients even before you start advertising. This way you will have a baseline of responses before you initiate the direct response advertising. This will prove to be a good comparison later on. You will also want to have an informational product to offer the listener, a tracking system that is in place before you start airing ads, a database to keep track of potential clients, and a system in place to communicate with potential clients at least monthly. Have this plan in place before you start advertising.

Keep in mind that once you actually begin your advertising campaign, every advertising sales representative (TV, Direct Mail, Newspaper, Outdoor Billboard, etc.) will be knocking down your door. Sales representatives monitor other media in order to find their own prospective clients. If you employ a radio-advertising consultant, then you can have them handle incoming offers. A business owner who is handling the radio advertising campaign himself might find it easier to not deal with these sales reps at all and simply tell them that they are not interested at that time.

Finally, it is effective to have one person assigned to lead the campaign. This can be either an outside consultant, or somebody in the office, but having a point person on an advertising campaign makes it easier to properly track the campaign, analyze incoming data and make the appropriate recommendations for the future of the campaign.

Here are some things to think about when setting up a direct response radio campaign.

What are you offering? You need to be offering something that potential clients find irresistible and compels them to make contact with you.

Is the URL or telephone number that you are using in your ads recognizable enough that somebody who hears your ad while driving will be able to remember it. It is crucial to have an easy to remember 800 number as well as an easy to spell, easy to remember URL.

Keep in mind your plan for when clients do respond. If you are referring the client to your webpage, never simply direct them to just the front page of your website. A better strategy would be to put in place a video on the page you are directing the client to. The video could act as a welcome to the potential client, and will really help you stand out.

Radio Ad Script Example (do not use):

Radio Ad Script Example

Boy, am I glad that the market crash is over, and that the markets will not go down again. Or will they?

Attention investors. If you have $500,000 or more invested, pay careful attention.

Get your free special report on how to bomb-proof your portfolio.

Hi, this is your local famous celebrity.

I urge you to call 899-222-3333 now to get your special report. Or you can search Bomb Proof Investing.com.

Call 24/7 899-222-3333 to get your free special report on Bomb Proof Investing. And we will also send you a free gift.

No one will call you, or answer the phone to try to sell you anything. I promise.

Having your life's work, your retirement nest-egg at risk makes me feel uneasy.

Call 899-222-3333 now to get your free special report, and we will also send you a free gift and a free sausage.

Protect your life's work, and your retirement nest egg.

Get Bomb Proof Investing now.

That's 899-222-3333.

899-222-3333 or BombProofInvesting.com

899-222-3333

Chapter 33
Maximizing Your TV Ad Budget

Television advertising is becoming an increasingly difficult medium for financial advisors. It is difficult to stand out among all the car and restaurant and other financial ads. It does not take a high degree of difficulty to produce your own ad, and there are more than enough ad agencies willing to insert your name into a standard formula advertisement and tell you to run that ad nonstop in order to put your name out there. Unfortunately for a midsize financial advisor, there are firms willing to spend millions of dollars on television advertising, all but drowning out the voices of those with fewer resources.

There are several problems with television advertising. The first is that there are often times hundreds of channels that people have the option of watching in their area. It is very difficult to identify where to spend your marketing dollars. Television commercials are also short. It is hard to narrow down which message you are going to convey in 30 seconds. The short length of your television ad also means that there is no guarantee that the viewer even saw it. For all you know, he might have been up going to the bathroom when your ad aired. Many people also have the option to fast forward through commercials completely if they own a TiVo or similar recording device. Despite this challenging landscape, there are ways for you to create a great television marketing campaign.

See how your competition is crafting their message.

Craft a different message from your competition.

Make the ad about the free, essential information that you are offering, and not all about your firm.

Create a unique phone number and URL in order to track the campaign.

Direct the potential client to a web page that is different from main page of your businesses website

Have a system in place for effective follow-ups once the prospective client has contacted you.

Most financial advisors fail to grasp that your advertisements have two main objectives.

Get clients

Build the ranks of clients and potential clients.

Some other useful tips:

Speak with a sales manager.

Have a system in place to track leads before the first ad even runs.

Make sure that the station works to your budget.

Write your own script. Does the station really know your business better than you?

Chapter 34
Celebrity

One method businesses use to raise their profile is by using a celebrity in their marketing campaign. A celebrity can inspire attention and help lower consumer resistance. Celebrities can also help your business's branding effort. The drawback to using a celebrity is that they are often hard to book, and even if you can book a celebrity for your campaign the cost alone may be prohibitive. Also be careful that they do not endorse you. The regulators will not be happy.

The great thing is you do not have to go out of your way to hire a celebrity. You should be the celebrity. It is possible for you to fashion yourself into the celebrity financial advisor in your geographic area.

Rebranding yourself as a celebrity is about getting a particular market, in our case people who are looking for a financial advisor, to see your presence everywhere they go. If successful, prospective clients will barely notice the existence of other financial advisors. You need to determine what your potential clients are looking for exactly, and how they are going about looking for it. When you have determined this, then you can develop the different ways that prospective clients can find you. Finally, you want to assist clients with learning more about you, why you are the best financial advisor for them, and how they can get in contact with you.

There are several strategies that you will want to follow in order to build celebrity status within your profession.

Websites – In order to build celebrity status, you will need to have more than one website. You will need at least one for your financial advisory business, one for you personally, and a blog. Other websites may be specifically geared toward media content, social media connection, and a whole host of other specified niches. Why adopt this strategy? Because Google, and other search engines typically will only show a website one time in it's organic rankings. The practical effect is that if you only have one website, you will only get one listing on Google. If you are trying to get your name out there, this is not ideal. If you have multiple websites then it is possible to get multiple listings. Multiple websites have the added benefit of showcasing multiple sides of you to a prospective client.

You do not have to divulge more of your personal life than you are comfortable with, but keep in mind that potential clients tend to like to do business with people they know, and consequently, can trust. Sharing stories about your life, or photos of your family, can be a great way for a client to really get to know you.

Most financial advisors advertising is so one-dimensional that potential clients have no idea who they are dealing with. This is a great area in which you can differentiate yourself.

Articles – Articles, like blogs, can also be used to drive up the relevancy of your website in a search engine search, so in addition to publishing them in hard copy you will also want to place them online. The Internet is content driven. The surest way to drive traffic to your site is to compile more relevant content on a subject. Articles are a great way to showcase your expertise to a potential client in an easy to process format. Articles, also like blogs, need to be kept short and actionable. Giving potential clients useful, practical information will keep them coming back and help you turn a potential client to an actual client.

Your articles can be longer than your blog posts, but do not feel as if they have to be. Make sure you include all the relevant information that you want to get across, but keep it slim. Your article should not act as a direct sales pitch. You are trying to build credibility with potential clients and they will not respect you if they come to you for information and all you offer them is a thinly veiled sales pitch. You want the article to offer useful and essential information. At the end of the article you can leave a byline that provides the reader with information on how to get in contact with you. If you are offering the reader new insights and useful tips, then they will be clamoring to do business with you. You will also want to add a link to your website. This will create additional inbound traffic and raise your profile.

Like blog posts, you are going to want to syndicate your press releases for wider exposure. For more on this refer to the chapter on public relations.

If you're utilizing keywords correctly, then you should start to see a marked improvement in your position on Google's main page. So, in addition to keeping your clients in the loop, you are also going to make your business even easier to find for potential clients.

Newsletters. What again?

Remember, while printed newsletters have been around for a while, they remain a highly effective form of communication. In its most boiled down form, a newsletter is simply just an assemblage of information packaged and processed in some digestible, entertaining way. You can choose to have your newsletter printed on high quality paper with color photos and a professional layout, or you can choose to print it in black and white. The most important thing to keep in mind here is that your objective is to draw attention to your business and remain in your client's minds. A newsletter allows you to communicate whatever information you want to your clients, whenever you want to deliver it. For more on this see the chapter on newsletters.

Outlined above are some of the best strategies for spreading information about you and your business to clients and prospective clients. These strategies also allow you to continue building your reputation as an expert and a reliable source of good advice. And of course, go back to the chapter on writing and utilizing your own book!

Chapter 35
"Freemiums" and Handouts

Free promotional items like mugs, pens and t-shirts can be a highly effective way to promote your business to COIs (they are good for COI relationship building, and are unlikely to sway a potential client, so don't send to them). Do not think of these items merely as handouts; rather look at them as advertising space. A pen emblazoned with your logo is a promotional item that is showcasing your message. (Do not confuse these with the client appreciation *gifts*—go back to that chapter to review.)

Some of the advantages to be gained by utilizing promotional items like these include:

Cost One thing that all financial advisors should be concerned with is the bottom line. How much do promotional items actually cost your business? If implemented correctly, promotional items should be a great return on investment.

For example, say you order 1000 date planners at a cost of one dollar each. You can incorporate information about your business directly into the planner. People find these types of products useful in their every day lives, and the planners are easy to hand out at a tradeshow or mail to a potential client. You have the ability to reach a large amount of potential clients very easily. If you end up signing only one client from this promotion, you have more than covered your costs.

Longevity If a person keeps your planner for a two-year period, and regularly uses it, they will be thoroughly inundated with your message. This goes for any type of promotional product. It is very likely that one promotional item will showcase your message thousands of times throughout its lifespan.

Visibility One advantage that promotional items offer over other forms of advertising is that they are typically repeatedly viewed. A newspaper ad may be only viewed once before being discarded and forgotten, if it is viewed at all. This problem is compounded if the person viewing your advertisement is not even in the market for a financial advisor. Not many firms have the capital to sustain prominent, long running advertising campaigns. Promotional items have the added benefit of keeping your name in the back of people's heads. Someone might not be in the market for a financial advisor for years, but when they do realize they are in need of one, they go to you first because they sip their coffee out of a mug with your logo on it.

Target Marketing Promotional items also allow you to selectively target the audience whom you want to receive your message. You are in control. Always try and target a specific market by giving them something that they will truly find useful and will appreciate.

Set The Tone When deciding on a marketing strategy, you may choose to run advertisements that are humorous in nature. Or you may choose the opposite and run ads that are serious and formal. In either case, promotional items can be adopted to enhance whatever advertising campaign you choose to adopt.

Improve Results Two things that every successful person has is a goal and a plan on how to achieve that goal. You need both of those things in order to successfully implement a marketing strategy using promotional items. Many business people make the mistake of ordering a promotional item without putting much thought into its use. For example, many people order pens thinking they are the ideal promotional product. They hand them out to their friends and family, but after that they are left without ideas on how to dispose of the rest of the pens. It is very likely that they will end up in storage or possibly even the landfill.

If you have a plan in place before you order those pens, then you are much less likely to reach the same result. Studies have shown that the use of promotional items in mailings produce better results than those without. Mail the pen with your information package touting your expertise as a financial advisor. Not only will you be giving them essential information, but you will also be giving them a promotional item they can actually use, and one that will keep you on their minds.

Chapter 36
Differentiation

In today's hyper-competitive, and understandably untrusting market place you need to differentiate yourself in order to be successful. If you are just another investment manager, another faceless financial advisor, there is no compelling reason a potential client will want to sign with you and your firm.

When you are thinking about your marketing strategy, you want to make sure that you are instilling in all potential clients an overwhelming desire to take and have what you are offering: You. So hone your story.

You want to communicate to potential clients the fact that you are unique. My own background? Here is my Public Relations Bio:

Mitch Levin, MD, CWPP, CAPP -- Financial Physician™

Two-Time National Best-Selling Author, Speaker, Trusted Expert

Widely recognized as a leading authority on the science of successful investing, Mitch Levin advocates on behalf of investors as well as their advisors. He is a Master Mentor for the Circle of Wealth, *Certified in Wealth Preservation Planning*; is an "AA" rated Florida State Representative of the *Asset Protection Society*; and is the Managing Director of Summit Wealth Partners, Inc. a federally *Registered Investment Advisor.*

When he retired as a prosperous eye surgeon, serial entrepreneur, and commercial real estate investor, Dr Mitch became heavily involved in the philanthropy world. He discovered the glaring need for process, clarity, transparency and full disclosure that all investors (large and small, sophisticated and novice) crave. Mitch sits on the investment committee of the **True Market™Models** to provide that solution, bringing comfort and confidence to your investment portfolio.

He has been featured in the acclaimed **documentary movie** *"Navigating the Fog of Investing"*, along with several of the most respected and accomplished Titans in the field, including **Nobel Prize winners.** In addition, he is the author of the **books** Smart Choices for Serious Money, and the newly released Science of Successful Investing Made Simple. He has also co-authored several other books (<u>GOAL: the Ultimate Survival Guide for the Profes-sional Athlete,</u> <u>Cover Your Assets</u>, <u>The Lies My Broker Taught Me,</u> and the two National Best Sellers, <u>Shift Happens</u>, and The <u>Power Princi-ples of Success</u>). Mitch has published hundreds of **articles**, and appeared on several **radio and television** interviews. He is featured on the **CD's** "The Seven Deadly Investor Traps", and "How the Really Smart Money Invests." Dr. Levin is a regular speaker: having given talks to thousands of surgeons, he also teaches fi-nancial advisors, accountants and attorneys across the country. Dr. Mitch is the also the publisher of the nationally subscribed news-letter, <u>The Rational Optimist</u>.

Interviewed as one of *America's Premier Ex-perts*™, he has appeared on **ABC, CBS, NBC, and FOX** affiliates, several podcasts, and radio shows. Mitch also has been featured in The **Wall Street Journal, Newsweek**, and **USA Today**, and several Florida newspapers, and medical professional journals, and is currently a **con-tributing editor** to HealthCareWealthCare™. His firm, Summit Wealth Partners, Inc. was recog-nized by **CNBC** ringing the NYSE opening bell, **Barrons** and **Forbes** and the **Orlando Business Journal.** Mitch has been a speaker in front of thousands of surgeons, and has provided brief-ings and education to financial advisors and some of the nation's largest and most presti-gious law and accounting firms. He is accred-ited to provide Continuing Professional Educa-tion Credits.

Dr. Mitch has presented:

How to grow your practice by helping your clients

Practice growth secrets of the most successful advisors

Pension Rescue -- How to restore the losses incurred in the last bear market

Tax Advantaged Wealth Building - Strategies of America's richest families

The *Extra* 7% Solution - How to increase investment returns prudently and avoid costly mistakes

Maximizer™ Investing - How to utilize the power of bonds to guaranty perpetual High income

Power ways to Invest for consistent and reliable returns, while controlling risk

Finding and stopping wealth erosions you may be unknowingly and unnecessarily suffering

"Mitch, thanks for a great evening. It was most informative and a great presentation"

-- Ray Watson, Chairman Vistage Florida - TEC Florida's New Name

"Dr Mitch is a passionate, knowledgeable, and caring interview guest, who touched on the topics all my listeners want to hear"

-- Wayne Kelly, Radio Host, Astral Media

"Dr Mitch was the most well prepared guest we've had. He was available, easy to work with, and provided great information"

-- Donn Burrows, Video Director & Documentary Film Maker, McGriff Media

Safe, prudent investing in today's dangerous environment; asset protection; fear of future unknown, government policy and regulation, and excessive taxation - these issues concern and affect nearly every successful professional and business owner. *"If you don't take out your own appendix, or represent yourself in a lawsuit, or fill out your own tax return, you are smart. So don't try to manage the complicated and dangerous and costly world of investing, tax management, asset protection, and wealth preservation without a qualified financial coach"*. Mitch's unique background assures that his interests are aligned with yours and your audience. This makes him a <u>much sought-after speaker and interview guest</u>. Remember, he does this because he wants to, not because he has to.

To Book an Interview, Call Dr Mitch at 866/977-2252 or email him at MLevin@MySummit-Wealth.com

While you are thinking about what makes your business unique, you will need to be developing information that will help you answer the question that is bound to come. "How are you different from all the other financial advisors. " or "Why should I hire you, and not the guy down the street."

Differentiating yourself is extremely important, and in order to reach your full potential as a financial advisor you will need to work on defining and proving the ways that you are different from your competitors. A good starting point is to sit down and list the skills and attributes which you feel differentiate you from your competition. Then you will want to search the internet and actually research what your competition is doing, and how it compares to what you have written down. At this point you will be able to see the qualities that truly make you special, and you will be on your path to differentiating your business from the rest of your competition.

Chapter 37
Niche Marketing

"The riches are in the niches."

Niche: a position particularly well suited to the person who occupies it

Niche Market: the subset of the market on which a specific product or service is focused

Niche Marketing: Concentrate marketing efforts on a specific and well-defined market segment

Marketing is a general term that incorporates various practices that are meant to enhance your brand and build your business through attracting and retaining clients. Niche marketing allows you to significantly narrow your focus.

As a financial advisor, niche marketing allows you to position yourself to meet the needs of a subsection of the market. This subsection can be a group, collection, or organization whose members have something in common so that their advisory needs are similar.

The level of specificity that you choose when defining your niche depends on the market that you are in. If the right individuals and assets are present, an opportunity to develop a niche market may be there.

Two of the most important variables for success with a niche market is that there are a large number of potential clients and there are substantial barriers to entry which keep other financial advisors from pursuing the market.

While many advisors view niche marketing as identifying a subsection of the population and pursuing that section with more zeal than they pursue other segments, it is much more complicated than that. To truly be a niche market, there needs to be a substantial barrier to entry.

When searching for a niche market, expand your horizon beyond the category of individuals with a certain level of assets. Every financial advisor is competing for these individuals. You want to be on the lookout for a segment of the population that has either been underserved or unidentified to this point.

Advantage of Niche Marketing

The riches are in the niches. Is your niche, like mine, the Middle Class Millionaire, a 58-year old business owner who has a net worth of $2-20 Million, most tied up in their business, and is concerned about the future? Or is yours the MD (this should be mine, see my article "Why business people think doctors are stupid"), or ATT executives, or the retiree, or is it the mass affluent?

A prospective client will not hire an advisor who is not in tune with that client's needs, problems, and goals. In order to make yourself a more marketable financial advisor, you will need to really research and gain insight into a particular group's needs.

It is difficult to find success as a financial advisor if you position yourself as a generalist. This is especially true if you are just starting your practice. The reason for this is trust. Potential clients need to trust that you know what you are doing and that you have their best interests at heart before they will hand their money over to you to manage.

If you are just starting out, then you have no track record on which a potential client can base that trust. Building trust takes time. Unless you have been in this business for over twenty years, and are constantly receiving more referrals than you can possibly handle, you should consider adopting a niche model.

Some of the advantages of adopting a niche model include your ability to perfect and more efficiently target your message to clients than your competitor who is a generalist. You are an insider, while your generalist competitors are outsiders. You also are able to consistently develop a pipeline of new clients.

The market for financial advisors is a competitive one. It is likely that you have numerous competitors who are experts in every subset of the population.

Having a target-specific practice is a great way to build your firm and also build your capability of helping clients whose particulars you will be in a great position to address. No matter what you call it, one of the best ways to grow your practice is by focusing directly on an available niche.

Become an expert in the needs of a niche market and you will have positioned yourself as the go-to guy when those potential clients are ready to hire an advisor.

Identifying a Market

You can make barriers to entry work to your benefit. They are the reason why untapped niches exist. Many people are of the opinion that a niche is too difficult to break into. Do not dissuade them of this opinion. Barriers to entry exist for all desirable niches, and they are to your advantage because they keep others out.

Marketing to the Niche

You will want to develop a marketing plan that is targeted specifically toward your niche. It is worth the extra time you will have to devote to doing this. While the plan does not have to be long or extensive, it will be extremely important to your overall success.

Once you have written down your plan you should read over it each morning in order to help you focus.

Now it is time to put your plan into action. Cultivating a niche takes hard work and determination. Making initial contact can come from many places. You may already have an in with an existing client. If not, then you will have to work at it. Call the company or hand out flyers. Identify key people within that niche. It may not be easy to get that initial in, but once you are in you will have a much easier time expanding your market.

The Multi-Pronged Marketing Approach

Once you have made initial contact, what do you do next? Once you have breached the niche market, you should:

Subscribe to all publications that are anyway related to the niche

Join any related club or organization.

Attend company meetings that focus on retirement issues.

You should be able to easily locate information relating to retirement plans. Unions will typically post them online, or you can obtain them from one of the employees of the organization that you are attempting to target. Once you have their trust, they will be much more inclined to help you. Remember that you are there to provide a service that the employees can choose to utilize or not. You are meeting a need. Your goal should be to:

Identify the niche.

Find a way inside

Join the club

Become an expert in their specific retirement plans

How to Conduct a Workshop

Yes they still work. It is more difficult to organize them and the results are lower than ever. And that is good for you. The barriers to entry are higher, and you are willing to jump over the barriers while your competitors are not.

Once you have found a way in, you should step up your efforts. Workshops are a very effective way to transition potential clients into actually being clients. The process of planning and executing an employee workshop is outlined below.

You should determine in advance how many workshops you want to sponsor throughout the year. After you have picked the dates for your workshop, you will be able to choose appropriate locations. Be sure to establish a primary location and a backup location, just in case something goes wrong and you are unable to use your number one choice.

What location you choose is dependent on the niche that you serve. In many cases a restaurant proves the perfect location to hold your workshop. This allows you to serve dinner while you are educating, and really helps build rapport with potential clients. Comfort and convenience are always important to keep in mind.

After you have booked a restaurant you can begin to create a menu for the event. Communicate to the restaurant's manager that you intend to hold these workshops on an annual basis, and they will likely go out of their way to be accommodating to you.

You should try and build a menu that offers at least a choice between three entrees. The prospective client will be able to order their entrée at the beginning of the meal. Because you are bringing in a large volume of customers, the restaurant is likely to offer you a discount price.

Once you have the details of your workshop set, you can begin promoting it. You should begin distributing flyers for the workshop at least six weeks in advance. Update your flyer each year, and tailor it specifically to workshop location and date. Your flyer will be used in several different steps of the process.

You will also want to send a direct mailer to prospective clients to inform them about the upcoming workshop. In the mailer you can include a letter, event flyers, and any other promotional items that you want to include.

Contact my office for access to a complete, done-for-you PowerPoint™ presentation to the retiree population, or any of several others.

Two weeks before the workshop, send out an email blast to all the prospects on your list. At this point you should be accumulating new prospects to contact from all the flyers you have been distributing.

About a week before your workshop, begin going out into the community and promote your event. Stop by the offices of existing clients, or go to areas where you think prospective clients will congregate. Plan to make 6-10 stops per day. At these stops you also want to distribute your flyer to get the message out.

At this point you should have a rough estimate of the amount people who will show up to your workshop. Make sure you inform the restaurant of the number of attendees you expect so that they will have ample time to prepare.

For the actual event, you want to create relevant promotional material. You may consider handing out your book, and other guides to selecting a financial advisor. This is also a great opportunity to give a gift bag . While there are "Marketing Gifts," gifts without your logo are real gifts of thanks. If you want to thank a client for signing up with you, send them a sweater or other type of gift without your logo.

Make sure that your actual presentation is long enough to get across all the information that you feel the prospective client needs, but is not overly long that they lose interest. Be sure that you find out the technical capabilities of your venue before you book. PowerPoint presentations are great, as are video presentations. Always keep in mind that the reason people are attending is because they want to learn more about your business.

Your presentation should cover the latest developments: Investment portfolio construction and expectations, new tax laws and how they affect your portfolio, Charitable giving until it hurts no longer applies™, how to calculate risks and fees in your portfolio, frontier markets, bond portfolios, Private Capital Reserve System™, Family Legacy Retirement Plan™, guaranteed income, taxes, inflation, health care costs, the Ultimate Gift™, IRA rescue, Intergenerational Guaranteed Income System™, the truth of costs and fees, how life insurance really works, and so much more. Contact my office for complete and compliant presentations that you can use.

Remember that when you are presenting to your niche market you are there to gain their trust, add some value to the experience, and convince your audience that you are the expert in your specific field.

In order to solicit more information from your prospective clients, you can have a drawing or giveaway. In order to enter the drawing, have prospective clients fill out a card that gives information that you find desirable. Have the prize be something that you can hand deliver, or make it something like a free dinner at a great local restaurant. This way you can show up to the event and connect even further with the prospective client.

The day after your event you will want to make contact with the prospective clients who attended. See if they have any questions, and try and schedule a time that they can meet with you at your office. If you are unable to make contact with them, go ahead and call them back the next day. After a week, if you still have not heard from them, go ahead and make another call. If still no contact, call them again after a month and then again at six months.

It is a good idea to invite prospective clients into the office for a complementary one-on-one consultation at least once per year. This gives you an opportunity to keep them up to date on the latest developments, but it also allows you to remain updated on any developments that might make them a more attractive client to you.

How To Get In The Door

In almost any market throughout the United State there is a company or organization that could be cultivated as a niche. If you are not able to find a niche than we suggest you try some of the following tips.

Contact your local Chamber of Commerce and ask them for a list of the largest companies in your area.

Do Internet research on companies in your location. You would be surprised how many large businesses there are around you that you had no idea existed.

Compare ideas with neighbors, friends, associates and people that belong to professional associations that you are a member of.

Actually go out into the community and knock on doors. Do not be intimidated to introduce yourself to local businesses.

It is not an easy task to identify new business opportunities. If it were, then everybody would be doing it. The barriers to entry may appear to be insurmountable, but with a little perseverance you will find that you can go far. You are providing a valuable service to the community. Studies have shown that people who invest for themselves typically fare worse than those who have a professional advisor invest on their behalf. You are also probably an expert in other fields such as insurance or taxation, and can provide valuable advice to prospective clients on these topics. People do not like to be lectured to, but they do appreciate receiving expert advice from a person they can trust. Read "Ten Minutes With Vito".

Chapter 38
Other Things to Consider

Watch Your Reputation

At the risk of sounding like a nag, never violate your clients' trust, nor impugn your integrity. You can and will do well by doing "good". In any business, integrity is a vital component of success. This is especially true in niche markets, which tend to be very interconnected. Be careful not to isolate anyone in your niche as this could lead to the loss of trust from the whole niche market.

Embrace Delayed Gratification

It is natural as a financial advisor to always want to be marketing to and advising clients. Keep in mind though, that delaying immediate gratification now will pay multiple dividends down the line if you are able to successfully identify and target an underserved or ignored niche market. They are out there and they are waiting for someone to discover them.

In these understandably untrusting times, the sales cycle has slowed to a crawl. Do not get discouraged. Keep doing the right things. Good things will happen. I promise. If you want more help, just contact me. We are happy to help.

Slow And Steady Wins The Day

Make sure that once you have identified a niche, you do not start out great and then taper off. Your ability to be a great financial advisor hinges on the ability to follow through. Always keep in mind the future that you want to have. You build trust with clients by consistently coming through for them. Always continue to market to your niche, even if you feel that you have done enough. Other financial advisors will be watching your performance and look for openings to the niche that you developed. Do not get complacent and let them in. Keep them away through stellar performance and always follow up with them. People have problems that you can help them with. You are the answer because you meet their needs.

Software For Database Management

Technological advances in database software have made it much easier for financial advisors to organize and track prospective clients. Software enables you to automate most of these processes. The most important tool that you have for tracking your niche market is customer relationship management software. Examples: Outlook™, ACT™, SalesForce™, RedTail™, Junxure™, and more.

Determine which customer relationship management software is the best fit for you and then make sure you train everyone in your office in its use. Your CRM software is essential to systemizing your business and running more efficiently.

Identifying Niches Takes Work

When you are searching for a niche market, do not just aim for the largest market that you can find. You need to seek a large market that has an unmet need. It might be better to sell hot dogs in the middle of a football stadium than to have a French restaurant in the middle of a desert. Why not sell to a starving crowd. What are your affinity groups?

Remember that when you are trying to identify a niche market, you want to be on the lookout for markets that are:

Underserved or entirely ignored

Have a large number of potential clients

Have a need that is not currently being met

Have barriers to entry

Have workers who are still employed

Have a decent retirement plan such as a pension or 401(k)

There may be a company just down the road from you who is in need of a financial advisor. Approach niche marketing with the mindset that you are in search of something that may exist in plain sight, but for whatever reason has been overlooked by your competition.

Once you have identified a suitable niche, create your marketing plan, work to overcome the barriers to entry, and do your best to corner the market. Follow this path, and the general market will be coming to you.

Chapter 39
I Am Relaxed!

We seem obsessed with money and power -- and then there is stress,, the stress that goes along with trying to have more money, and time and a better, larger practice. We ignore our quality of life. So, as a result, we've created stress and burn out and it's now becoming an epidemic, according to industry experts. Remember, Ariana Huffington collapsed from stress on what should have been a high point in her career, when she sold the Huffington Post to AOL for $350 million.

It's a little ironic that while I am sitting here on the beach in Longboat Key, I am talking to you about stress. But it's a part of our lives. The latest scientific research shows that increasing levels of stress and burn out have consequences not only for our personal health, but also on our healthcare system.

Carnegie Mellon found that from 1983 to 2009 there was between 1 and 30 percent increases in stress related illness throughout all demographic categories. Research in Massachusetts General

Hospital in Boston estimates that between 60 and 90 percent of doctors' visits are regarding stress related conditions and conditions like heart disease, which are also related to stress, are increasing on a year over year basis.

Clearly, the way that we are leading our lives – what we prioritize and what we value – is just not working today. Adhesion conducted an RIA stress survey. 58 percent of respondents rated stress on the job as important. While only 48 percent rated enjoyment of what we do as an eight or better. We are just not having as much fun.

Although 2013 was good for the equity market and our business, 53 percent of respondents indicated significantly increased stress levels. So, clearly it's time to change the way we do business.

According to Bob Veres' latest research, hundreds of respondents admitted problems with burn out and stress. And they offered other very specific suggestions and solutions focused on improving the lives of financial advisors.

The two most commonly cited sources demanding mental overhead that consumes your time and are the sources of significant stress: 1) managing your back office operations and 2) managing investment portfolios.

The research is pretty clear; we've become far too focused on our back office and we retain the misconception that clients view our value specifically regarding our investment management skills.

The number one reason clients leave an advisor is poor communication, while, investment returns ranks only 8th on the list. Veres says, "Advisors are struggling under the growing weight of managing their back offices. What took between 10 and 20 percent of their time, now is over 40 percent and unfortunately they don't have time to do the part of the business that they enjoy most."

It is not just the part you enjoy most. It is the part of the business you are best at and your clients want the most.

A "front office approach" allows you to put more focus on your clients. It's the reason most of us got into the business in the first place. So why not engineer a business model that supports this and allows you to focus on those clients?

There are additional methods to using the more front office approach, too. One of the characteristics of happy and successful RIA's is that their principles spent significantly *more time on client facing activities*. Re-structure your business so that it actually allows you to focus more time on adding client outreach – and actually return that time to your clients.

The research also suggests that advisors who have that front office approach --moving from managing investments *to managing well*, have increased profits by over 35%. Surveys show that we as advisors add more value for our client relationships by just keeping them, hanging on to them, making the sure the "back door" is closed, than we do by picking the best investment managers, or providing incremental returns.

By keeping your clients engaged in your plan, the client will experience more success, and you will likely have more success, too. This isn't to say that the investment proposition is insignificant. We all know that's not true. Rather, there are solutions that can help free you up to step into the *Wealth Manager* role, that allows affluent clients to get from you what they expect. Being a wealth manager is a differentiator. It's extremely important.

Delegating, or outsourcing your investment management and back office (which after all, are cost centers) are great ways for dealing with the stressors as they creep up.

There are other ways for dealing with stress on a more personal level. One of the most important is setting boundaries between your business and your personal life. Be committed to time with family and make sure to develop a work/life balance and actually prioritize it. Put it into your schedule and honor that schedule.

Why not carve out an afternoon or a day to get away from the routine of the office. Think of it this way: on Thursday, golf is good. I have been doing this myself since the day I opened my doors in 1985. It's therapy. It's okay. Your clients even want that for you. Your family certainly does. And isn't that one of the reasons we are in this business?

Many of us have very set, firm guidelines on the types of clients, account cycles and fees that we are going to accept. Those guidelines allow you to focus on your business and -- on your client.

You already are intentional about the way that you shape your business. We want to help our clients achieve their outcomes.

Instead, are you spending time, "losing sleep", about reconciling accounts, or worrying about your business disaster recovery plan?

Focus more on your clients through better time management and outsource. Outsource your investment management. Outsource your back office. We think that's important. Take more of a wealth management approach. You want to take away anything that takes you away from your client. Be more intentional about organizing your business and your life.

Chapter 40
CONCLUSION.

I know that you are busy, and there are a million things you could do besides reading this book, but you have made a wise investment in your future. There are two reasons why I wrote this book. One is to educate you and the second is to encourage you to establish a mutually beneficial relationship with us.

I suspect that won't surprise you. You want to work with people that you know, like and trust, people who have your interest at heart, people who are going to help you achieve more with your time, earn more money and sign more clients, because we all know the world does not need another money manager.

What qualifying advisors will get from us, in addition to solid core strategic modeling, is a suite of marketing tools and tactics that can help you grow your practice.

Go to www.TrueMarketModels.com/suitemarketing.

Heraclitus said, "Nothing endures but change," and change in the markets is normal and good. Consider adapting, developing, and enhancing your core-satellite approach and have True Market™ Models handle the core portion of your clients' portfolios.

Here are your benefits:

As a multi-asset class, global, actively strategic indexed ETF fund manager, you will get diversification and transparency, you will get efficiency, and you will get *powerful performance*. And while so many others *say* that, maybe some people deliver it as well. Yet our models have beaten the blended benchmarks (comprising the Barclays Aggregate and the MSCI All Country World Index) for the last 12 years by 1% to 2%. It's easy to use and easy to access on the Overlay Managers, like Placemark and Envestnet, and others. Just ask your custodian.

But in addition to that, we are also advisors' advocates. We know exactly what you want. You want your clients to excel. You also want greater income, more time, and more clients. We make it our mission to help you achieve that. The less time you spend on identifying fund managers, the more time you have to develop client relationships. The less concern your clients have about portfolio overlap, the more your clients will stay with you.

We guaranty integrity, transparency, and accountability.

True Market™ Models work very well in the core/satellite approach for those of you who spend a lot of time and effort managing your own tactical portion of the portfolio, or for those of you who don't believe in the tactical portion, or for those of you who use third party managers for the tactical piece.

These core strategic models work very well in conjunction with tactical, satellite investments. There is little to no overlap; the models are highly efficient -- tax efficient, cost efficient, time efficient. They are easily understandable and easily explainable -- even to someone who shows little interest in, or whose eyes glaze over when discussing money, investing, or numbers. Your clients will thank you for knowing exactly what's in the portfolio and why. That can make all the difference in the next generation staying with you.

Managed ETF's are among the hottest part of the new wave of investing, because of transparency and efficiency. We all know that mutual funds report on what they had on the last day of the quarter, but who knows what they had in the other three months of that quarter? With ETF's, every single day you can see what is in that portfolio.

Our Active Strategic Indexing™ of ETF asset management provides transparency, efficiency, minimal overlap, and low turnover. It been said that in the 401k space, within 10 years 90% of assets will be held in Exchange Traded Funds.

True Market™ Models are designed for the advisor who really wants to grow his business and they are designed for the client who is looking for solid growth that is safely managed.

Here is one example of some of the added value:

You can have your own book right now, "*The Science of Successful Investing Made Simple*" with your photograph on it and your name on the cover.

If you don't want to write anything, you can present it. If you choose to write an introduction, and we can help you with this, the book can be introduced by you. We have got a template for that. There can be a forward, an epilogue or a conclusion by you. Again, we've got templates for that. Or we can help you rewrite or add a chapter or two or three so that you can be a co-author of this book.

Download your free special report now. How Top Performing Advisors Get to the Top and Stay There

You can take this book *The Science of Successful Investing Made Simple* and turn it into a series of articles. Then put these articles in your specialty exclusive trade journal.

If you specialize in manufacturing, there's a manufacturer's trade journal. Because every business owner is looking for the same thing we all are looking for, more time, more money and more business.

Many business owners finally come to the point where they recognize that their own business is merely a micro-cap illiquid high beta stock and with so much of their net worth tied up in their business, we all seek the ones who are looking to diversify their asset base and their income stream. (See my upcoming

book, *"PAYDAY! Your business sold. You have Sudden Wealth™.*
Now What?")

So we wrote some articles, put them in trade journals and here
is an example of who came to us as a result, in the medical
doctor niche. A surgeon came to us who does $7 million in
gross revenues, and takes home $3 million a year. This man just
became a client.

You work hard to earn your clients trust. We want to give you
time and to give you the resources to grow your practice. We've
got a plan to help you, and a plan that helps your clients. It
is transparent and we've got accountability. All this adds up to
trust and making you a better advisor.

We can help **you grow**. And you get to **keep your Independence**.

Be Better. Do Better™

Make Great Decisions™

Appendix:

Get your Free Gift: A special report on Best Practices for Financial Advisors

www.TrueMarketModels.com

EPILOGUE

One Degree of Separation

One degree of separation can be the difference between success and failure in these proven, trust based financial advisor marketing strategies. You have probably heard about the concept of how to boil a frog. You know, put the frog in a pot of tepid water and slowly raise the temperature. And that concept works to a point. The difference in one degree is the difference between 211 degrees and 212 degrees Fahrenheit.

James Watt transformed the world into the industrial revolution by understanding this one degree of separation. By creating steam merely by adding one more degree of temperature to the water at 212, the steam engine was born. It is that one degree difference that made the engine go.

None of the strategies and techniques in this book are easy, although they are simple. Your success can depend on just adding one more degree of extra energy and the success will start to overflow. Here is to your success.

ACKNOWLEDGEMENTS

"There are no new ideas. There are ideas that have been left unfulfilled by lack of action"

Many have spoken or written on various and similar topics before me. These include Ben Glass, Dan Kennedy, Scott Hanson, Pat McClain, Bill Johnson, Matt Zagula, Steve Moeller, and so many more. If you have read them, some of this may seem familiar. No one has synthesized it all into one volume, and who has actually done it. No one has written how to grow your practice after the great financial meltdown. Those are the reasons I wrote this book.

Some who inspired and encouraged me to write this: Nick Murray, Don Blanton, Jay Conrad Levinson, Harry Beckwith, Bill Glazer, Chet Holmes, Financial Planning Association, Ari Galpar, TD Ameritrade, Fidelity, Placemark, AssetMark, Global View, and countless financial advisors, accountants, insurance agents, and other service providers, we have counseled over the years.

And, many thanks to the investment advisor representatives, financial advisors, registered representatives, insurance agents, annuity agents, independent broker dealers, independent registered investment advisors, independent marketing organizations who daily work hard to help your clients. It is because of you that we will make the world a better place, one investor at a time.

Many thanks to Summit Wealth Partners, Inc.; to Vicki Brodnax and to Kyle Levin, JD for his brilliant editing and for keeping me on track, for helping me write and complete this. On time, too.

Mostly, I wish to thank our clients. Without you, there would be no reason to help other advisors help other clients. It is our mission to empower full financial health. We believe this will improve the world, one investor at a time.

ABOUT THE AUTHOR

Mitch Levin, MD, CWPP, CAPP, The Financial Physician™ graduated from Beloit College with a degree in English Literature in 1976. Afterwards, went to work in the Harvard Graduate School department of surgery computer labs under the Chief of Surgery, then attended SUNY Stony Brook School of Medicine, where he developed his interest in financial matters and was instrumental in setting up, what may be the first and completely student-financed long-term endowment campaign through insurance and derivative products.

In the early 2000s, Dr. Levin retired from active practice of medicine to devote himself to philanthropic endeavors and to his family. It was during this period, he became increasing interested in financial matters and investment Ultimately, this led him to begin a new career in the field of wealth management and he became "The Financial Physician™" and CEO of Summit Wealth partners, Inc.

Dr. Levin is certified in Wealth Preservation Planning and Asset Protection Planning and is an "AA" rated Florida State

Representative of the Asset Protection Society. He is a two-time national best-selling author, trusted advisor and accomplished public speaker.

His published works include a multitude of professional articles and papers, as well as the books *Power Principles for Success; Goal!, The Financial Physician's Ultimate Survival Guide for the Professional Athlete; Shift Happens; Smart Choices for Serious Money;* and *Cover Your Assets: How to Build, Protect and Maintain Your Own Financial Fortress*

You may contact Dr. Levin at mlevin@mysummitwealth.com